A
Single Eye
of
Light:

Sacred Visions
(Poems & Letters)

By Ronne R. Gleason

Cover By: Morris

Graphic Layout, Text Layout, Typing and Design by;
Donald H. Mac Donald Jr.

Printed in United States by;
Morris Publishing
3212  Hwy 30
Kearney, NE  68847


Gateway Books
1439 N.W. 25th Place
Cape Coral, Florida  33909

## Acknowledgments

As I absorb inspiring sensations from nearly everyone I encounter, it would not be possible to list all sources of inspiration and learning that are contained within these works.

The teachings of Gurdjieff, Ouspensky, Gold and the Holy Fathers of the Ancient Eastern Christian Orthodox Church have been a constant inspiration to me. I am particularly thankful to Donald Mac Donald Jr. for the laborious task of typesetting and laying out the manuscript. Since poems and letters have been addressed personally under pseudo names, I'd like to thank these people for the inspiring moment.

Because  the Athletes at Anchor Bay High School have inspired several of the poems; I am also indebted to them for not only the skills displayed (Both female and male players are a true joy to watch) but also for the ebullience and energy they tender to each and every play!  No finer adult entertainment can be had than at a Local High School.

Picture of Author in his home

I Would like to dedicate this work
To my parents who inspired me
to carve my destiny
And to accept me as me!

Picture of Author's Parents
Drawing in graphite 11x17
Titled : Mom & Dad
(1995)
By Ronne R. Gleason

# Table Of Contents

# Table Of Contents

# INTRODUCTION
## A Single Eye of Light: Sacred Visions Poems & Letters

All to often in our search for meaning in our lives we travel hither and thither eyeing the visible at the expense of the inner wealth we've inherited as humans. The Poems and letters contained, herein, churn out the inner folds of one's being. Several poems use metaphors to reveal hidden meanings in phenomenological occurrences in everyday life. Some poems paint a tapestry of my spiritual quest to stem the tide of base passions early in life. I exploit the virtue of paradoxical wording to dissolve opposites juxtaposing a feeling of centeredness in the reader. As these feelings transport one further into his/her personal abyss, discord may rupture one's sense of reality; but suddenly a rhapsody of harmony greets one's inner being; a calmness ensues. Due to the interior nature of the poems and letters, a careful reading is required to derive maximum benefit however.

A central most theme of these writing(s) is that one must rise above one's natural impulses of the body that entrap SOUL; that cripple's our God given potential to not only Sculpt Soul into a true likeness of God but also to maximize our Creative Potential. A body given over heedlessly to the lower passions is a spiritual crime against God and all of His spiritual Co-Workers in the INVISIBLE WORLDS as we, unwittingly, surrender our right to experience the Wonders and Splendor of the Kingdom of God Within; "MADE WITHOUT SOUND OF HAMMER!"

II    References are made throughout the poems and letters that explain THE VALUE OF RETAINING THE SEXUAL FLUIDS our true cement to build the temple made without sound of hammer, "[THE TREE OF LIFE]." Jesus refers to this substance as the "Golden Oil." Needless to say, one who surrenders to the Natural Impulses of the Body(temple), thereby expelling these Gigantic Temple Builders (semen-seed-ojas-cerebro-spinal fluid) SURREPTITIOUSLY paves a highway to hellish detours, thereby making the road back home to God unnecessarily prolonged and painstaking. As some poems intimate, INTENTIONAL suffering-voluntarily going against the natural impulses of the body, isn't suffering at all as promised by our Father in Heaven and Lord Jesus " As my burden is light and My yoke is easy" whereas, UN-INTENTIONAL suffering is mere meat for a life besieged by UN-wanted suffering i. e. the common malaise of our human condition! "Take up the cross and follow me" Jesus admonishes, but ears of deafness, stuffed to the brim with a life of merrymaking, ravage the earthen plains coyly seduced into thinking a life "WITHOUT WORK" is acceptable as long as faith is present in the seeker. Imaginal faith is spiced soup for the slothful; for the un-disciplined! Real Faith is the motor that propels one to heed the value and virtue of a life sparkled by IN-tentional suffering; indeed, a life wherein the "Burden is light and the Yoke is Easy!"

I use comedic paradox to vouchsafe that seriousness is the password for the miserable and Non-seriousness (buoyancy of spirit) is the heritage of the wise! Consider a simple rose

flower emits a heavenly fragrance; a Busied mind, so <sup>III</sup> overwrought by its Outer beauty, attempts to touch its stem and dissect the wherefore of its magnificence, but gets pierced by the thorns in the process; A Lightened (or should I say an En-lightened) spirit merely accepts the fragrance in all of its simplicity inhaling its inebriating aroma! A philosopher (or foolosopher dances between the thorns, hoping not to get picked while a Mystic catches the drift of the aroma and flies off motored by the fragrance of one of God's Tentacles called a mere Rose Flower! A philosopher has to scratch his head, whereas God scratches the Mystics head. A philosopher chases God; A mystic LETS GOD CHASE HIM AND PRAYS HE GETS CAUGHT! Thank God for free will; it's our choice to chase or be chased.

When you know in your heart that what you see in the outer is a mere reflection of that which has already manifested itself on the panoramic screen of the invisible world you develop a penchant for observing external life's countless situations in the form of waking dream symbols. For example, If I see a muffler setting alongside the road while driving, I immediately reflect, did I speak harshly to someone recently. In other words, since mufflers are made to quiet the sound of vehicles, I deduce from this symbol that the Universal Mind or God is telling me to put a muzzle on my mouth. Nothing is outside of God's view and He commences to teach us in most mysterious ways. Numerous waking dream symbols can be accosted in one's personal life situation if ATTENTION to the outer world is imbibed without MECHANICALNESS!

WONDERFUL SECRETS IN GOD'S UNIVERSE CAN BE
DISCOVERED BY ANYONE IF THE NORMAL
AUTOMATED ATTENTION FOCUS IS ABORTED!
Lower animals are mechanical and automated to survive as per
God's will, but humans are afforded the mighty gift of free will
TO DEAUTOMATE the human biological machine while on
earth so that we may secure alignment with the heavenly forces
in the spiritual worlds upon death to the flesh body. In its utter
simplicity, ATTENTION for more than a few minutes. is
difficult (i.e. maintain one thought without the invasion of
other thoughts) as the world of outer delights has so pampered
us, that non-mechanical patterns of behavior is a rarity. As
some may think they have a right to respond negatively to any
given situation, why not ponder the Non-Mechanical reaction
of One Has A Right "NOT" TO RESPOND NEGATIVELY
no matter what the situation!

A true student of life will not only develop his or her
skills in deciphering-decoding God's mystery symbols (as above
so below the microcosm inside the macrocosm) but will also
enjoy the harmonic ride back home to God! A SINGLE EYE
OF LIGHT: Sacred Visions, appropriates this glorious
phenomenological occurrence with not only Mystical allusions
but also the grounded day to day phenomena. My joyous
attendance at a local high school's athletic events even serves
to bridge the gap between the Visible and Invisible worlds. As
several of my poems suggest, even in sport, wonderful
discoveries along the bridge linking earth to heaven can be
made.

As you ponder the poetic rambling(s) I hope to not only titillate your philosophical questionings(s) but also to stimulate your unequivocal penchant for introspective Irrationality!

---

Young people don't need sex education, they need guidance on how to capture passions, before they capture them. Who amongst us can teach this wondrous art; (sublimation of sex energy) if none; then don't tinker for the stream of hormones gurgles just waiting for direction; any direction will do for a young impressionable mind; nature cringes at the possibility of a void saying fill me; fill me; any, any dab will do; circumcise the passions not the organs. Meanwhile fill this ravenous cup of nature with this psalm as admonished by the early church fathers of Christian orthodox "Come to my help, oh God! Oh Lord, hurry to my rescue!" Circumcise the spirit and 'watch' the body follow as you repeat, over and over through the day, this special powerful prayer.

Preface
Visitor From
Afterlife

The setting for this poem is the ethereal terrain of the afterlife. Afterlife on earth. The initial plane encountered is the astral plane, a region of intense emotions and colorful rays. Because emotions color our astral body (notice the aura surrounding the flesh body) the residue of these colors engraved onto THE ASTRAL BODY'S A U R A during our earth life live on and the negative emotions are seen as brownish-grayish and blackish tones on the astral plane by the disembodied or departed soul. White, yellow and violet are the spiritual colors that are engraved on to the aura during earth life providing a life of virtue and chastity was imbibed. Unless one has clairvoyant vision while on the earth, one can only see these aura colors once they have entered the afterlife. No personality can mask one's degree of spiritual development in the higher world. In other words, the departed soul is an open book for others to see, i. e. even misshapen faces sculpted onto the astral body are observable. The astral plane is the first region of God's mysterious kingdom of Heaven(s)!

The speaker in the poem is the departed spirit (soul) who eagerly tries to communicate his or her sensations of flight amongst the inhabitants of this wondrous Kingdom of Heaven!! The deceased meets with apostles who provide classrooms in learning of these heaven worlds. Angels and spiritual travelers instruct soul how to respond and manage all SENSATIONS EGO goes through via P U R G I N G itself of all the earth dross. Erewile, soul vacillates between joyous feelings it once felt for its mate still on earth and the splendorous sensations experienced in the heaven worlds. Ego's residue, coloring the astral body, is wrenched, as it wrestles with glorious sensations as it encounters the cleansing vibrant rays and heavenly melodies. Encountering h e l l beings (see quatrains numbers 73,74) soul is buffered by the guiding hands of spiritual travelers, angels of light and the apostles. They aim to steer soul away from hazardous encounters.

The reader learns that though their departed or deceased mate is swirling in space; in flight like a bird without wings as there is no gravity in the higher world, many experiences are had as the law of karma (cause and effects of one's actions good or bad "you reap what you sow,") rears it face onto the panoramic screen of soul; the picture painted being one of ugliness or beauty or combination of the two depending upon the benevolent or malevolent acts exercised while still on earth. Ego still wants to cling to old earth passions like a gnat to a swan. "Come bathe with me, my love, else my heart will rankle like a razored knife," is an example of this. (See quatrains 64 and 65 in the poem.)

The poem suggests that truly loving lifetime couples on earth, will reunite in the heaven worlds!! The primer for this allusion is the numerous references soul (deceased) makes to his beloved mate still on earth. Indeed, still trapped on earth, as the kindly hand of God's woven web, has not yet taken his or her soul to His Garden of Eden!!! The deceased tries desperately to convey this message to his earth mate.

The theme of the poem can best be realized if the reader understands what Paul, the Apostle, meant when he said "I DIE DAILY." The secret reference here is the "Tenth Door" or "SINGLE EYE" spoken of by Jesus. (See quatrain 46.) In other words, Paul could leave his flesh body at will thus enabling soul to enter the heaven worlds and he could return to earth at will, also. Having the foreknowledge of one's own heaven world plight is invaluable to the deceased and vouchsafes the virtue of the statement of the saints "DIE BEFORE YOU DIE." This poem lends some insight into the journey we must all take some day before we die or after death.

It's our choice.  Jesus says "SEEK AND YE  SHALL FIND."  Indeed, the window
to the heaven worlds is in this "Single Eye."

**1**

DEAR LOVE, I'VE COME TO EASE YOUR PAIN;
NOW A GHOST BUT I SEE YOU CLEAR;
YOUR THIRD DAY MOURN GRIEVES ME MORE
WHILE I HOVER ABOUT THE CELESTIAL PLANE.

**2**

PLEASE  WALK ALL YOUR REMAINING DAYS
WITH SPIRITS REACHING TO THE SKY;
THE PULSE OF YOUR HEART IS MY PULSE TOO.
YOUR TIME IS NUMBERED TO MEET ME ANYWAY!

**3**

PLEASE FREE YOUR SORROW FROM MY GRIP
BEFORE YOU SINK TO SLEEP IN OUR BED.
YOUR BREATH'S INHALE IS MY EXHALE.
AGAIN WE'LL MEET: YOUR LIP TO MY LIP.

**4**

PLEASE GIVE YOUR HEART TO ANOTHER TENDERLY;
UP HERE AMONGST THE LUMINARY'S
I LEARNED THE WISDOM: THE JOY OF SHARING;
ANOTHER BEAU WILL BE LUCKY LIKE ME.

**5**

WAY DOWN THERE, MY DEAR LOVE,
YOU WERE MY SAVIOUR FROM ON HIGH;
MY GIFT TO ANOTHER IS YOUR FREEDOM FLIGHT;
THE MESSAGE COMES FROM HIGH ABOVE!

**6**

OOP'S, SOMEONE'S KNOCKING ON MY DOOR;
I THINK IT'S ONE OF THE APOSTLE'S,
HE WANTS ME TO ATTEND HIS SELF PRIDE CLASS.
ME SO PROUD AS WE WALKED IN THE STORE.

## VISITOR FROM AFTERLIFE

### 7

THEN I'LL ATTEND HIS EGO CLASS.
MY LOVE, YOU MADE ME FEEL MAJESTIC.
THE BEST OF THE BEST O'ER ALL THE REST
EVEN WHEN YOU NAGGED ME TO CUT THE GRASS!

### 8

TO ME SHE'S MORE THAT A WIFE.
OH LORD, SO BLESSED; SO LUCKY; WHY ME?
THE MERE CHANT OF HER VOICE QUIVERS MY SPINE;
YOU LOANED ME A PARTNER WHO W A S MY LIFE!

### 9

I PONDER: HER BEAUTY GREW WITH AGE.
THE SCENT OF HER HAIR; THE SCENT OF HER BODY;
THE TOUCH OF HER EYES; THE CARESS OF HER LIPS;
SHE WORSHIPED ME MORE THAN A SAINT ON STAGE.

### 10

TEETER TEETER OH PRIDE! OH PRIDE!
YOU ARE MY FRIEND; YOU ARE MY ENEMY;
TWAIN THE TWO I'M LEFT ALONE
WAY UP HERE WITHOUT MY BRIDE!

### 11

OOP'S, A KNOCK ON MY CABIN DOOR.
I QUIP, WHAT NOW DO I HAVE TO UN-LEARN?
SO MANY MYSTERIES UP HERE IN HEAVEN;
VICES TO BLOATED TO FIT THROUGH THE DOOR.

### 12

AS I THOUGHT, IT'S THE APOSTLE JOHN AGAIN.
HE WANTS ME TO ATTEND HIS GARDENING CLASS.
AS YOU KNOW, MY MIND WAS A SWAMP;
IDEAS UN-PRUNED WILTED IN THE DEN.

### *VISITOR FROM AFTERLIFE*

**13**

SURELY, STRANGE WAYS ABOUND UP HERE.
UPSIDE DOWNSIDE ALL TWISTED UP
THE TERRACE OF MY MIND IS FULL OF WEEDS
BUT MEMORIES OF Y O U BRING ME CHEER!

**14**

MY DEAR, NEW THOUGHTS TO COME; JUST THINK:
IF I PASS THE GARDENING CLASS
MY HEAD WILL EMPTY; TWO THOUGHTS REMAIN:
MY LOVE OF GOD AND THE GLOW IN YOUR WINK.

**15**

A GLOVE AND A GRIN AND A EMBRYO TO SPROUT;
A GARDEN TO HOE TILLING UP THE CRUST
WEEDS ARE STUBBORN; THEY WERE BORN THAT WAY;
NO QUICK FIX, I NEVER HEARD YOUR SHOUT.

**16**

PONDERING: YOU NEVER SCRATCHED YOUR HEAD.
YOU JUST DID AND A HUNCHING YOU'D GO.
I WAS BALDING WHILE YOUR HAIR LUSTERED;
YOUR SPIRIT BUOYANT I WEIGHTED LIKE LEAD.

**17**

A MIRROR IN MY FACE YOU WERE TO ME;
SMUDGES SMUDGES I DIRTIED THE MIRROR;
MY MESS MY MESS YOU CLEANED UP AFTER;
THE MAN IN THE GLASS I COULDN'T SEE.

**18**

TO YOU, MY DEAR, THIS MESSAGE I GIVE:
NEXT DOOR TO YOU I AM RIGHT NOW;
THE DANCE OF DESTINY IS OUR ENDOW.
BY CHANCE YOU MOURN I DIED TO LIVE!

### 19

THE  EMBRYO WE BORN IS PREGNANT WITH LOVE.
GRACE AND MORE GRACE IS IN OUR CUP;
MY \*S I L I V  E R    C O R D HE CHOSE TO SNAP
BUT TASTE THE HERBS IN OUR VESSEL FROM ABOVE.

### 20

SO WONDROUS THIS KINGDOM INSIDE;
MIGHT PROPELLED BY GOD'S LOVING HAND;
THE TAPESTRY'S GLIMPSE BLOATS MY SOUL;
THE TABLET UNSEEN IS INKED IN STRIDE.

### 21

SO MANY LIGHTS, THEY COLOR MY SIGHT;
FOREVER ANON CAN THEM I BASK!?
SHADES OF BLUE; SHADES OF GOLD;
OH GOD! AM I WORTHY OF SUCH HEIGHT?

### 22

THEIR BEAMS ALL OVER EMANATE A HEAT;
EGO'S IN FRIGHT OVER A WHITE BEAM PIERCE
ITS COATING SHIVERS FEARING ITS SHED,
IT SHOULD, CUZ IT'S THE DEVIL'S MEAT!

### 23

AND THAT IS PENNED IN HOLY WRIT;
DUST UNTO DUST IN THEE I TRUST..
S U B T L E BODIES GOD MADE FOR FLIGHT;
HIS MANY SPHERES SO NEATLY KNIT.

### 24

JUDGEMENT DAY, I AWAIT A NEW SLATE.
ANOTHER GO AROUND ON THE \*\* WHEEL?
THE AMBER OF TIME KNAWS MY PATIENCE';
BUT TEMPLATE OF COSMOS CHALKS MY FATE.

\*Silver cord connects soul to body. \*\*Wheel of many lifetimes.

### 25

THIS *BARDO PASSING, A BETWEEN LIFE TEST;
STRUGGLES SWELLING THE FACE OF EGO
NEARS ABLUTION; MY GHOSTLY BODY
STILL LONGING TO FEEL YOUR THUMPING BREAST.

### 26

WHY ME THE FIRST TO PART OUR SHIP?
ALONE I AM WITHOUT YOUR GLANCE,
YOUR LUSTER LOCKS AND GRABBING EYES.
I LONG FOR THE CLASP OF YOUR GRIP.

### 27

JUDGEMENT OF MERCY OR JUDGEMENT OF WRATH;
MY **AKASHIC RECORD SPINS AND RECORDS;
THE LAMP OF DESTINY IS IN YOUR HANDS;
PLEASE DEEM ME WORTHY OF YOUR PATH.

### 28

A FLASH BACK TRANCE I FALL INTO;
WHO WILL TAKE OUT THE GARBAGE CAN?
I MISS MY HOUSE ITS COZY FROLIC;
I MISS THE KIDS THEY MADE ME TRUE.

### 29

OOPS, A KNOCK ON MY DOOR;
THINKING IT WAS ONE OF THE APOSTLE'S,
A NOTE I'M HANDED; THE SCRIPT IS WRITTEN:
YOUR JUDGMENT IS MERCY JUST AS BEFORE!

### 30

MESSENGERS OF GOD, ALL OVER THEIR VOICE;
THEY FLANK ME BELOW AND SIDE TO SIDE;
THEIR CHEERY ROBES FLUFFING IN SPACE;
THESE ANGELS OF LIGHT ECHO MY REJOICE!

* Bardo passing is the period (forty nine days) between lives we spend purging karmas i.e passions.
** Akashic record is the memory bank of our life on earth and the higher planes.

### 31

*BEETHOVEN AND WAGNER WOULD EVEN REJOICE*
*AS ECHOES DANCE TO EDEN'S SONG?*
*BRINGING SHIVERS THROUGHOUT THE REGION;*
*STILL, MY LOVE, I LONG TO HEAR YOUR VOICE!*

### 32

*SO MANY SOUNDS ALIEN TO EARTH;*
*SO MANY VOICES IN GOD'S ORCHESTRA;*
*THEY MOTOR THE HEAVENS, THAT I KNOW!*
*HOWLING HUMANS BLOT OUT THEIR BIRTH!*

### 33

*\*MELODY ONE THROUGH MELODY FIVE;*
*I'M STRUCK IN AWE BY HEAVEN'S CASCADE;*
*MY \*\*COVERING GONE EXILED FROM BONDAGE;*
*I GOBBLE AND GASP THE AMBROSIA I THRIVE!*

### 34

*I SWIRL ABOUT NO WINGS OR LUNG;*
*I TRAVEL BY WHIM MERE FLICKERS OF THOUGHT;*
*REFULGENT SPLENDORS CONSUME ME;*
*THE SECRET ELIXIR I TASTE WITHOUT TONGUE!*

### 35

*I HEAR THE MUSES WITHOUT MY EARS';*
*I SPEAK TO MY BRETHREN BY CLOSING MY LIPS'*
*I'M OVERWROUGHT BY AROMAS WITHOUT MY NOSE;*
*I GLIDE;. MY EYES ARE DINED BY TEARS!*

### 36

*FLOOR DANCE TO SKY DANCE, I AM NOW HOME.*
*THIS KINGDOM'S NOT METER NOR MILE AWAY,*
*NOR OVER YONDER; IT IS WITHIN!!*
*WITH FEET TO EARTH I KNOW YOU ROAM.*

*THEIR ARE FIVE KNOWN MELODIES HEARD ON THE HIGHER PLANES.** COVERING
MEANS FLESH BODY.

### 37

*MY LOVE, COME VISIT, IT'S IN THE SCRIPT;*
*EACH WITHOUT EYES; WE'LL CUDDLE OUR GAZE*
*BUT ONLY FOR A SHORT WE MUST ACCEPT*
*CUZ YOUR DAYS ON EARTH ARE STILL UNSTRIPPED.*

### 38

*MOURN ME NOT, CELEBRATE YOUR FLIGHT,*
*RECALL THE INSTANT OF OUR GAZE;*
*CHERISH FOREVER, THAT IS OUR WINE.*
*CELEBRATE GOD AND HIS KINGDOM'S MIGHT!*

### 39

*MERCY BEFORE WRATH NO MORTAL CAN DOUBT.*
*THE WISDOM OF AESOP COMES TO MEMORY;*
*SLOW AND STEADY WINS THE RACE;*
*BEARING UP THE CROSS WE'LL WIN THE BOUT.*

### 40

*INSIDE THE TEMPLE PASSIONS QUELL;*
*NO BOULDER OF \*SISYPHUS CAN TOPPLE YOU DOWN*
*AMID THESE LIGHTS AMID THESE SOUNDS*
*LIKE LEAVENING BREAD YOU'LL RISE TO THE BELL.*

### 41

*LIKE LETTUCE IN A COLLANDER I SOMETIMES FEEL;*
*TOPSY TURVY I DANCE AND TOPPLE;*
*MEMORIES OF EARTH KEEP RINGING, KEEP SPINNING*
*LIKE BAIT ON THE END OF A FISHIN' REEL.*

### 42

*NO GRAVITY TO GROUND ME; VOID IS MY SPACE;*
*THE MYSTERIES ARE CRYPTIC, INDEED THEY ARE;*
*THE MASTER JESUS, PARABLES HIS TOOL,*
*I AM GOD INFECTED TO MEET HIS FACE!!*

\*SISYPHUS WAS KING OF CORINTH. SISYPHYS' SON GLAUCUS WAS FOREVER
SUMMONED TO ROLL A STONE UPHILL WHICH FOREVER ROLLED BACK DOWN UPON
HIMSELF BECAUSE HE BETRAYED A SECRET OF ZEUS.

### 43

*THESE REGIONS CELESTIAL, THEIR RAIMENT INTOXICATE;*
*GOD KNOWLEDGE BECOMES MY DUE INCLINE;*
*HEAD NO MORE TO BURY IN THE SAND;*
*I MOURN EVEN THE LOST SCENT OF A LILAC'S FATE.*

### 44

*EGO'S MEANDERING AMONG THE PHANTOMS;*
*MY EARTHEN FARE, ONLY YOU, MY LOVE*
*WERE REAL TO ME; YOUR LOSS I MUST BEAR*
*ELSE I'M LIKE A STOMPED CHRYSANTHEMUM.*

### 45

*THE WINE WE SHARED ITS ESSENCE LIVES;*
*IT LIVES ON AND ON FOREVER ANON';*
*SWEET DESTINY'S WEB KNOWS WE ARE ONE*
*FOR GOD ETERNALLY ETERNALLY GIVES!*

### 46

*DURING OUR MOMENTARY CUDDLED GAZE,*
*CONNECTION ETHEREAL WE MERGED AS ONE;*
*TEMPLES SHEDDED SO FLIGHT CAN ENSUE*
*THE \*TENTH DOOR OPENS QUICKENING OUR PHASE.*

### 47

*VIEWING GOD IN THE REFLECT OF YOUR EYES*
*I KNEW RIGHT THEN OUR EARTHEN UNION*
*WAS NO QUICK FIX TO CANDY OUR PLATE,*
*INSTEAD A CLUE TO ABANDON ALL LIES.*

### 48

*FOR KNOWING THYSELF IS KNOWING THY SOUL*
*FOR THROUGH THE FATHER WE'RE SURELY ONE;*
*SELVES MERE SEEDS TO BORNE THE TREE;*
*WRATH, OH NO, WE PAID THE TOLL!*

\* Tenth door is the third eye or single eye spoken of by Jesus located between the physical eyes a slight above the brow line.

### 49

*CONSUMED BY YOU, YOUR HEART IS MY HEART;*
*YOUR BREATH, MY LOVE, IS TOO MY BREATH;*
*WE PULSE IN CADENCE THE \*ASTRAL PUNCTURE*
*NO BODIES TO DRAG OR FALL APART!*

### 50

*MY ADORATION BREATHLESS EVEN UP HERE,*
*BUT I WRITHE AS A BIRD STUCK TO A BRANCH*
*HEARKENING YOUR VOICE TO SET ME FREE*
*STILL BEDEVILED BY EARTHEN CHEER.*

### 51

*OH GOD! OH GOD! YOUR CHECKERBOARD QUILT,*
*YOUR HAND DIVINE HITHER AND THITHER;*
*I WORSHIP YOUR MUSE NOT TO AMUSE,*
*OR IS THAT A LIE THAT SATAN BUILT?*

### 52

*MANY MANSIONS UP HERE, MY EYES MEANDER;*
*MY MORTAL DRESS AND SLIGHTED CUP*
*WEIGHTED THE BALLS AND SHORTENED THE CHAIN*
*FORSAKING DIVINITY CUZ I DIDN'T UNDERSTAND HER.*

### 53

*EGO'S BEHEST, ERRANTLY BEDECKING,*
*CHECKMATED ON THE SQUARES NUMBED BY MAMMON,*
*EARTH MY BOG BUT YOU, MY LOVE,*
*FLOATED EVEN WHEN WE WERE NECKING.*

### 54

*HEAVEN ON EARTH, THAT WAS OUR BREW,*
*NOT CUZ OF ME BUT CUZ OF YOU,*
*DULY FRAUGHT WITH PRECIOUS WARES*
*YOU LIVED FOR ME, NO FURTHER ADIEU!*

* Astral puncture is the penetrating of each other's astral body i.e the subtle body that surrounds the physical body approximately eighteen inches out from flesh. This astral body lives on after death and is a vehicle for flight in the higher worlds. And is punctured during intercourse.

### 55

*KINGLY MIGHT I THOUGHT BY BOAST;*
*MY FOUNT WAS POOR AND YOU KNOW WHY.*
*BEYOND ALL PRICE YOU ARE MY PEARL;*
*SWEET DESTINY SWEET DESTINY MAKE YOUR TOAST.*

### 56

*GOD IS MY LEAVEN; NO DOUBT I HARBOR*
*BUT YOU ARE MY BREAD, BREAD OF LIFE;*
*ERE ENDLESS PLIGHTS IN REGIONS CELESTIAL*
*I STILL FANTASIZE WE'RE UNDER THE ARBOR.*

### 57

*THIS BARDO PASSING OVERWHELMS THE SOUL.*
*WANDERING BEINGS DEPARTED LIKE ME;*
*PENETRATING RADIATIONS, VIBRATING COLORS*
*KEYED TO DISSOLVE THE PASSIONS TOLL..*

### 58

*THEY COWER HANDILY, THESE PURGING RAYS';*
*JESUS IS LIGHT, HE SAYS SO I KNOW;*
*REVELATIONS GIVE HINT, BUT LO, HE'S COY;*
*HE NEVER REVEALS HOW THEY CLEANSE OUR WAYS;*

### 59

*STILL THE STRUGGLE GOES ON AND ON;*
*MEMORIES OF EARTH SEEM FROZEN IN TIME;*
*EGO ITS FLARE AND BOTTOMLESS FLASK*
*CLINGS SO TIGHT LIKE GNATS TO A SWAN.*

### 60

*CRYSTAL WATERS ALL AROUND AND AROUND,*
*FLIP AND FLOP I'M SWIRLED ABOUT;*
*TO NUMB TO REACT TO THE HURRICANE FORCE;*
*I'M BATHING IN THE PURIFYING SOUND!!*

**61**

*THE EDDY OF MY FLIGHT AN ENORMOUS TASK;*
*GRAVITY ONCE REAL TRIES MY MEMORY;*
*\*BODY WAS MINE THAT TOO A FALLACY;*
*NOW CHIMES AND LIGHTS ARE MY BASK.*

**62**

*IMAGES SEDUCTIVE BUT STILLNESS MY REFUGE;*
*THE\*\*SHORES OF GOD A SIGHT TO BEHOLD*
*TANTALIZES EGO OBSESSED BY GLITTER.*
*UP HERE, EGO IS TRULY A STOOGE.*

**63**

*I LONG FOR THE FAMILIAR, SHADOW OR NOT;*
*\*\*\*HABITS, IF GOOD, WILL GUIDE ME THROUGH;*
*THE APOSTLES TAUGHT ME IN GARDENING CLASS;*
*I TRUST IN GOD HIS MYSTERIOUS PLOT!*

**64**

*ALL THESE\*\*\*\*CHAMBERS; ALL THESE COVES;*
*WHERE IS MY DEAR, MY LOVE ON EARTH?*
*MY HEART RANKLES LIKE A RAZORED KNIFE*
*MISSING HER GAZE AT THE YONDER GROVE.*

**65**

*COME BATHE WITH ME, NO SOAP OR TEAS;*
*CRYSTALLINE WATERS ANOINT MY TUB;*
*ETCH YOUR NAME ON IT AS WE WADE,*
*WE'LL MERGE AS ONE LIKE MILK IN CHEESE!*

**66**

*THE ASTRAL BLEND; NO BODY TO LOOM;*
*THE SCARF OF EARTH'S DREAM DROWNS;*
*THE MIRTH OF YOUTH, ITS WINE, SUBMERGES*
*GOBBLED ALL UP BY GOD'S IMPUNE!!*

* Body is not ours... ; it's god's temple given as a vehicle for transformation. ** Shores of god or 12 known regions in God's Heaven Kingdom. ***Habits good i.e practicing virtues on earth , not head knowing.**** Various purging stations in higher worlds that we must all pass through.

### 67

OH VANISH! OH VANISH! WILL O' WISP.
LET THIS BATH LAST FOREVER;
NO TEMPLE TO CLEAN NO TEMPLE TO GROOM
EGO'S KNAW NO LONGER CRISP!

### 68

BUT LO! OH GOD, THE *SERPENT LURKS;
MY FALL TO SIN MY PREDESTINATION;
CHASTISE MY WHIMS ENAMORED BY EARTH;
MY **VINE THE TRAIL AWAY FROM THE PERKS!

### 69

***RESERVOIR THICKENS WITH OIL OF GOLD***
GYRATING UPWARD TO MEET THE LOTUS*****
BASKING IN THE MANNA OF THE VINEYARD WATERS******
A CELIBATE'S REWARD HIS JOY TO BEHOLD!

### 70

OH VANISH! OH VANISH! EARTHEN LOT;
LISTEN LISTEN TO MY SOUL'S REVERB!
SLAY THE TONGUE OF THIS COILED VIPER,*******
I CANS'T NOT LOSE THE PRECIOUS WHITE DROP!!********

*Serpent is a coiled energy force sitting at the perineum or muladhara chakra situated below spine between anus and sex organ.

**Vine is the tree or spinal column and connecting ganglia or branches. Tree of life or the Strait says Jesus.

***Reservoir storage of sex fluids normally plucked up during intercourse situated in muladhara chakra and pineal center or third eye region set between eyes a slight above brow.

****Oil of gold referenced by Jesus. The precious life elixir or essence commonly referred to as semen.

*****Lotus The thousand petalled lotus or crown chakra that blossoms during enlightenment.

******Vineyard waters cerebro spinal fluids-sex fluids retained not spent-wasted during intercourse.

*******Coiled viper-serpent situated in sex or muladhara chakra readied to uncoil ere placing intense attention on same. Kundalini yoga practices this method. Attention at third eye is safer enabling one to bypass the potential ravenous sex urges associated with the kundalini fire.

White Drops: Sperm.

### 71

*THIS BODY OF CLAY I SCULPTED WITH GOLD*
*DURING MY STAY ON SATAN'S EARTH;*
*MY HEAVEN SOJOURN SO MUCH TO LEARN;*
*REGIONS GALORE WITH SAINTS OF OLD!*

### 72

*\*SPIRITUAL TRAVELERS MANNING THE TILL;*
*LUMINARIES OF THE SKY THEY LIGHT MY WICK*
*LENDING THEIR NUDGES TO MY FLYING SOUL;*
*THEIR VENERABLE GUIDANCE MAKES ME STILL.*

### 73

*AMONGST THE WAILS OF \*\*HUNGRY SOULS*
*THE FIRES OF PURGATORY FRY THEM HELPLESS;*
*LIFE'S GREAT PURPOSE THEY NEVER PONDERED*
*THINKING BASE EARTH A GIANT CANDY BOWL!*

### 74

*TO THIS I'M WITNESS: KARMIC IMPUNE*
*DURING MY HOLDOVER ON THE BARDO PASS,*
*MISSHAPENED SPIRITS WAILING AND GRABBING,*
*TESTING MY WEAKNESS FOR SATAN'S TUNE.*

### 75

*INDIFFERENT TO THEIR SONG AND BELL,*
*MY POSTURE OF STILLNESS STARVES THEIR EFFORTS;*
*THANK GOD FOR APOSTLES, THEIR CLASSROOMS IN THE SKY,*
*THEY TAUGHT ME THE METHOD TO QUELL THEIR SPELL;*

*Spiritual travellers are guides we encounter upon the earth to direct us to regions suited to our development.
**Hungry souls: Disembodied spirits still craving earth pleasures. Passions energized by desperate souls. A chaste earth life eases ones passing through this plane unscathed.

*76*

*DELIGHTS OF THE \*ASTRAL CAN TRICK ANY SOUL,*
*BUT SOULS MUST BEAR THE FURNACE TREATMENT*
*AS PASSIONS MUST SETTLE TO ENDURE HIGHER REGIONS;*
*HERE LIES THE TEST OF \*\*KAL'S SECRET SCROLL!*


*77*

*KAL WORKS FOR GOD, MERCY HIS PLOY;*
*HE RIPS AND TEARS THE SUTURES OF EGO*
*FOR PAIN AND MISERY ARE EGO'S FESTER;*
*HIGHER REGIONS NO ROOM FOR THIS FEEBLE TOY!*


*78*

*MERCY MERCY BEFORE ALL WRATH!*
*THE WEAVER'S HAND HEARTILY AT WORK;*
*THE FLAMES OF EGO MUST BURN THEIR COURSE,*
*ERE SOUL CAN SURVIVE THE ASTRAL BATH.*


*79*

*EGO'S DRESS ADORNED TO PUFF;*
*SWIRLING ABOUT LIKE TUMBLE WEED*
*HAS MET THE WEAVER HIS ANOINTING HAND;*
*MY\*\*\*ROOF TRICKLES AWAY ALL THE STUFF!*


*80*

*SOUL'S RESIDUE ON AUTO PURGE;*
*ANGELS GUIDE ME TO THE NEXT CLASSROOM;*
*THE APOSTLE'S WORDS ARE ONLY FEW*
*BUT THEY CHURN YOU LIKE A POWER SURGE!*


*81*

*COMPASSION IS WRITTEN ON HIS D O O R.*
*HE ASKS: "CAN YOU PLUCK OUT YOUR EYES*
*TO GIVE, WITHOUT FLINCH, TO A BLINDED MAN"?*
*"IF CANNOT DO THEN EXIT MY STORE"!*

* Astral plane: first plane encountered upon death to physical body and harbors countless disembodied spirits boasting unfulfilled earth passions. It's the lowest of higher regions and is energized by intense negative energy. A chaste earth life creates a protective aura around soul easing the pass through this plane of hazard.  ** Kal the Name of Satan's force. Kal Nirangan. ***Roof :Brain.

### 82

*MORTAL FLARES RANKLING MY THOUGHT;*
*MEMORIES OF MY LOVE, OUR CRYSTALLINE BATH,*
*LINGER BUT WITH VISION GONE;*
*CAN I CUDDLE HER GAZE AND BE OVERWROUGHT?*

### 83

*BUT LO! I RECALL THE HOLY WRIT:*
*"IF THINE EYE BE SINGLE LIGHT WILL FILL ME"!\**
*THIS EYE IN THE CENTER, ITS HEAVENWARD GAZE;*
*PLUCK OUT MY EYES I TRUST THE SCRIPT!!*

### 84

*MEMORIES ONCE FROZEN MELT IN BITS;*
*SWEET BIRDS CHIRPING ON THE GANGLIA OF THE VINE*
*TANTALIZE MIND ITS FOLLIES ON EARTH;*
*HOW EGO IS MEAT FOR EARTHLY SKITS!*

### 86

*YOU BLESSED ME THOU; I FOUND YOUR DOOR,*
*THE \*\*SECRET TENTH THE WINDOW TO HEAVEN*
*THE GARDEN WOVEN BY A MASTER WEAVER;*
*COME, MY DEAR, MANY REGIONS TO EXPLORE!!*

### 87

*I'M OFF THE WHEEL OF ENDLESS LIVES;*
*TO YOU, MY DEAR, I'M NOW A GHOST.*
*BELIEVE BELIEVE, I LIVE ON AND ON.*
*MY KERNEL INSIDE, PERFECTION IT STRIVES.*

---

\* Single eye spoken of by Jesus. It's the third eye or pineal gland located between eyes a slight above brow. When opened or softened brings light and sound.

\*\*Secret tenth: same as third eye or single eye.

*88*
*HOLY SPIRIT! HOLY SPIRIT!*
*YOU ARE THE TENTACLES OF SOUND AND LIGHT;*
*MY CUP IS TURNED RIGHT SIDE UP;*
*FERRY MY COURSE WHO ELSE TO STEER IT!!*

*89*
*YOU BLESSED ME THOU! TENTACLES FROM THE ETHER;*
*GLAZING MY EYES WITH WATERS OF JOY;*
*I SEE WITHOUT SIGHT; I FEEL WITHOUT LIMBS;*
*A G A I N, MY LOVE, WE'LL BE TOGETHER!!!*

(A satirical expose ' of man's artifice buried beneath his/her divineness)

*As an elderly man asked me, "How do I think"? I responded accordingly: If God placed His formula for thinking in a bottle materializing this bottle right in your lap, would you open the bottle? The elderly man was wise, and said NO! I quipped, "Then why do you want to know how I think"? He laughed and agreed, sensing my humor in the joking remark. I further elaborated thus: "The spark of God's thought reverberates in all of us, no matter what our station in life, no exceptions!"*

*Though I would not open the bottle deciphering Gods formula for His Grand Thought, for I believe blindness to the future is kindly given so we can fill the circles marked by heaven, I do, however, know He thinks in patterns of opposites, metaphors and satire. It's the coordination of opposing patterns, pluses, minuses, positives, and negatives that create the foundation for a THIRD FORCE! This third force is a neutralizing energy pattern i.e. the fields that create light in a common light bulb and more supremely, the mother earth! Sun is positive in nature while the moon is negative in nature and the union of the sun and moon borne the earth. Though the earth is bound by gravity, we are, inexorably, privy to experience ZERO GRAVITY! When we experience the union of internal positive and negative energy fields within our TEMPLE we have sensations of our soul exiting our flesh body, even with eyes open, namely, an out of body experience. It has been said, from time immemorial, that humans are Third Force Blind!.*

It's not within the scope of this poem to explore this phenomenon in depth. However, by reading and pondering the satirical couplets presented in this poem, an automatic perusal of positive and negative thought patterns are invoked. A third force is felt upon comprehension of the couplet where a sense, not so common, is realized, namely, laughter, or simply a feeling of Yeh, that's right, will come to the surface.

The verses are spaced sporadically, intentionally, for in actual life situations, events happen adventitiously with no coherent connection. Yet, beneath the surface runs a SUBTLE silken thread that kneads; that weaves a profound matrix; indeed, a WEB of our destiny!

A GLOVE (negative) AND A FINGER (positive)
AND AN EMBRYO (third force neutralizer) TO SPROUT:
A FINGER CUT IS A FINGER ON THE MEND! !

Though this verse is not as starkly inverted as the verses contained in the following pages, it does, however, boast of the three forces at work in Nature; A SIMILE if you will, of how the COSMIC PLAYWRIGHT REVEALS TRUTHS TO US!

# PARODY; "THE CRITIC"

*In the midst of a contusion their is a solution.*

### I DREAMT OF YOU OR WAS IT ME?

*Brother, Sister, where have you been?*     **1**
*So long, so long, to hear from your pen!*

*In the pool of folly your double play;*     **2**
*So also for me, our real forte.*

*You barbaric buzzard; You common fly;*     **3**
*I dreamt you were a wizard dancing in the sky.*

*You molting insect and mental brute:*     **4**
*I dreamt you escaped while playing your flute.*

*You carnal dork and popping cock;*     **5**
*I dreamt of your poverty and humble stock.*

*You bellied brain and bulging gut;*     **6**
*I dreamt of you fasting meditating on your butt.*

*You empty shell and bulging heart;*     **7**
*I dreamt of your soul, its kindly fart.*

*You barren carcass and cussing voice;*     **8**
*I dreamt you Sainted by Pope Paul his choice.*

*You defecating factory and mucoid cud;*     **9**
*I dreamt you were a weed, with a flower BUD.*

*You coughing lung and spitting gnat;*    **10**
*I dreamt of you flying like a hungry bat.*

*You bombastic heathen with tilted skull;*    **11**
*I dreamt you a God, transcending your bull.*

*You preaching machine and air filled tongue;*    **12**
*I dreamt you were a cow who sheds no dung.*

*You well read parasite from books you hold;*    **13**
*I dreamt you were aged, selling them for gold.*

*You thinking corkscrew and fiendish brain;*    **14**
*I dreamt you were an angel and mind without stain.*

*You stenchy swamp and weed laden mind;*    **15**
*I dreamt you were empty, no one could find.*

*You noxious goblin and babbling clod;*    **16**
*I dreamt of you MUZZLED, TALKING TO GOD!*

*You mechanical automaton in a rat-borne maze;*    **17**
*I dreamt you rut-less, no need of a raise.*

*You clumsy boaster and prideful glut;*    **18**
*I dreamt you were a Master, converting a slut.*

*You cackling guzzler and boisterous drunk;*    **19**
*I dreamt of you sleeping with God in His Bunk.*

*You pretentious farce and puffed up head;*      **20**
*I dreamt of you headless, yet face all red.*

*You hygrade phony with plastic smile;*      **21**
*I dreamt you were valvoline, purging the pile.*

*You fancy thinker with words that trip;*      **22**
*I dreamt you mindless, with no handle to grip.*

*You empty cauldron garbed in pomp:*      **23**
*I dreamt of you naked, with no suit to stomp.*

*You conniving baboon always on the take;*      **24**
*I dreamt you wealthy, with no gold to bake!*

*You gossip bomb and slandering twit:*      **25**
*I dreamt you converted; TO HOLY WRIT.*

*You useless hand and thoughtless knave*      **26**
*I dreamt you a mercenary and monastic slave.*

*You wimpish mat and brownie upper;*      **27**
*I dreamt you were a King, with Jesus at Supper.*

*You dodging duck and yapping joke;*      **28**
*I dreamt you enlightened by the COSMIC JOKE!*

*You snarling rodent and painted mask;*      **29**
*I dreamt you starving for God's Great Task!*

You sense driven goat and palsied fool;          **30**
I dreamt you were chaste, kissing God's Stool!

You self pitying nuisance and barren punk;          **31**
I dreamt you were an Angel, Slaying the Bunk.

You soothsaying worm and squirmer for loot;          **32**
I dreamt you BLINDED BY SOUNDS OF THE FLUTE!!!

You demonic magician with mixtures of fright;          **33**
I dreamt you HALOED BY GOD'S WHITE LIGHT!!!

You worldly huckster and pampered snook;          **34**
I dreamt you cloistered, curled under a book.

You impassioned flesh-head bee-lined to hell;          **35**
I dreamt you chanting, manning the BELL!

You raucous Libertine and driveling Horse;          **36**
I dreamt you Cele(Bating) your chastened course!

You Hypo'd-crite with shameless squawk;          **37**
I dreamt you wise, walking your talk.

You polished zombie and social sham:          **38**
I dreamt you a hermit, munching a yam.

You greedy miser with buried coin;          **39**
I dreamt you penniless, with cloth over your loin.

*You pedantic showman and pulpit stooper;*   40
*I dreamt you were a director, unveiling a blooper.*

*You forlorned brood with saddened brow;*   41
*I dreamt you cleansed, by the forest's prow.*

*You pampered stud with no bone in your spine;*   42
*I dreamt you Towing, THE ENTIRE LINE!*

*You faint of heart and shifty parasite;*   43
*I dreamt you A stand Up, with dare and might.*

*You sated pig with fork in your beef;*   44
*I dreamt you FULL UP,  with a carrot leaf.*

*You legal beagle with coy in your tongue;*   45
*I dreamt you were a rancher, shoveling dung.*

*You Nut House Doctor with pills to pop;*   46
*I dreamt you were a mortician, cleaning up your crop.*

*You parroting intellect with (UN) hallowed words;*   47
*I dreamt you tongue(less), feeding the birds.*

*You well schooled snob with haughty style;*   48
*I dreamt you homeless, sleeping in your bile.*

*You libertine(d) lethario and bopping tramp;*   49
*I dreamt you baking, at a nunnery camp.*

*You dreamy capitalist with finery you love;*     **50**
*I dreamt you in a tent, at peace like a dove.*

*You hapless winer sulking in your rafter;*     **51**
*I dreamt you mixing, A POTION  FOR LAUGHTER.*

*You Fortune Teller with a buck to clasp;*     **52**
*I dreamt YOUR FUTURE BECAME YOUR PAST.*

*You clairvoyant inebriate foaming at the cud;*     **53**
*I dreamt THEIR THOUGHTS BECAME YOUR MUD!*

*You married roasters and teaming trifle;*     **54**
*I dreamt you alone, Thanking God For LIFE!*

*You solitary griever and friendless nerd;*     **55**
*I dreamt God was your FRIEND and not the herd!*

*You concurrent collector of the commoner's pulse;*     **56**
*I dreamt you without antennae, in an ancient cave.*

*You possessing monger with a controlling gear;*     **57**
*I dreamt you in Flames, with love in your tear.*

*You ignoble dullard straining the air;*     **58**
*I dreamt you a butler, scenting a chair.*

*You painted damsel and dressed up liar;*     **59**
*I dreamt you a cotton weaver, in a nun's attire.*

You societal elect with brazened tongue;    60
I dreamt you a cuckold, falling flat in dung!

You heartless Jack lumbering your bales;    61
I  dreamt you a gardener, with dirt in your nails.

You packing rat with piles high;    62
I dreamt you in flames, with no more to buy.

You clocking grappler with life tick(ed) away;    63
I dreamt you a pendulum,  SWINGING AFTER THE DAY!

You clocking cleaver with life tick(ed) away;    64
I dreamt you a pendulum, SWINGING BEFORE DAY!

You clocking wort, time worn to death;    65
I dreamt you a pendulum,  swinging after your last
breath!

You clocking (RUT-STER) in haste for the chime;    66
I dreamt on your death bed, you asked for the time.

You cigar toting fool on a roll at pool;    67
I dreamt you choking, sucking on stool.

You adultering rake flirting your twig;    68
I dreamt you reborn, Married to a PIG!

You formal plate and royal fork;    69
I dreamt you splattered, while popping the cork.

*You pimping Lard and searing sleeze;*     **70**
*I dreamt your organ, dropped off from a sneeze.*

*You political Zit and ranting dreamer;*     **71**
*I dreamt your notes, blotted in the steamer.*

*You healthy body with vital frame;*     **72**
*I dreamt you killed, by a drunken dame!*

*You guzzling glut and hobbling wince;*     **73**
*I dreamt you lived, forever since.*

*You chastened monk with vital lymph;*     **74**
*I dreamt you baited, by a \*Celestial nymph!*

*You horny cuss with dangling brain;*     **75**
*I dreamt you anointed, by a castrater's cane.*

*You complaining snot with fevered head;*     **76**
*I dreamt you levitating, on your sickened bed.*

*You rambling bigot with puffed up sense;*     **77**
*I dreamt you slayed, for a six pence!*

*You corny cackler with worn out dreams;*     **78**
*I dreamt you uprooted, in a field of streams!*

*You twelve hour slave, you're tempting Death;*     **79**
*I dreamt you penniless, before your last breath.*

\*Angelic being in the heaven world with beauteous radiance not seen on earth.

You misered hog with silkened blood;                    **80**
I dreamt your BOX , washed away in the flood.

You political gloater with boring wit;                  **81**
I dreamt your bubble burst, soiling the carpet!

You friendly cajoler with dice in your Rap;            **82**
I dreamt you Gambled away your chap!

You air-waved cork broadcasting your likes;            **83**
I dreamt your Wine, flooded the Mikes!

You guru hopping beebop with glitter in your eye;      **84**
I dreamt you a zookeeper pampering a fly.

You ashram hopping beebop with ideas in your way;      **85**
I dreamt you a hangman, decapitating your prey.

You Holy Writ parrot slithering in your chirp;         **86**
I dreamt you in your cage, humbled like a twirp.

You fame seeking glut with pride in your grin;         **87**
I dreamt you a well-digger, with walls caved in.

You coiled viper pregnant with hope;                   **88**
I dreamt you miscarried, falling down the slope.

You grunting owl with stubborn propose:                **89**
I dreamt you Wise, WAITING GOD'S DISPOSE!

*You possessive ogre dead in a crux;*  **90**
*I dreamt you crushed, between mack trucks.*

*You slippery worm tunneling to skirt;*  **91**
*I dreamt you surrendered, coughing up your dirt.*

*You snorting rhino with lust in your gaze;*  **92**
*I dreamt you stomped, and slurped like mayonnaise.*

*You taunting monkey and bully(ing) brawler;*  **93**
*I dreamt you gutted, like a night crawler.*

*You well mannered cuckold with smell in your mode;*  **94**
*I dreamt you a skunk, sniffing your Load!*

*You hybrid druggie with diamond(ed) scarf;*  **95**
*I dreamt you choking, on your barf!*

*You market timing fool primed to win the race;*  **96**
*I dreamt your car crashed, trying to out pace.*

*You cheetah flying speedster with quick way to God;*  **97**
*I dreamt you were a turtle, beating the hot rod!*

*You master Astrologer with stars on your brain;*  **98**
*I dreamt a COMET, exploded in your train.*

*You master palmist with lines in your brain;*  **99**
*I dreamt you a butcher, with hands ground to the vein.*

*You Master-ologist with creosote in your breath;* **100**
*I dreamt you a Stump, water-logged to death!*

*You master magician with flare in your knack;* **101**
*I dreamt your gown, got fried in the ACT!*

*You master comic with slander in your speeches;* **102**
*I dreamt you smothered, by a Hoard of Leeches!*

*You gossip columnist with harm in your tongue;* **103**
*I dreamt you a TOILET, SWALLOWING THEIR DUNG!*

*You master historian with nostalgia in your purse;* **104**
*I dreamt you a \*woofo-woofo bird, flying in reverse!*

*You philandering geek with your caravan of whores;* **105**
*I dreamt you crashed, into your wife's car door.*

*You virgin nun with God on the run;* **106**
*I dreamt (HE caught you), without borning a son.*

*You virgin monk with God your Fun;* **107**
*I dreamt you survived, without your gun!*

*You preacher man with collections on your mind;* **108**
*I dreamt you a beggar, of coin for the blind.*

*You preacher man with an eye for a star;* **109**
*I dreamt you a caddy, filling up your jar!*
*\* Ancient bird that flies in reverse.*

*You childless lady that sowed like a worm;*     **110**
*I dreamt you gave birth, without the sperm.*

*You God-Seeking soul with fear in your sigh;*     **111**
*I dreamt you Found HIM, when you covered your eye.*

*You ambitious beaver with riches as your goal;*     **112**
*I dreamt your collar burned, frying your soul.*

*You church going devout who seemed on the level;*     **113**
*I dreamt you kissing up, to the Devil!*

*You graying old man with stories to tell;*     **114**
*I dreamt you Longing, for the ring of a school bell!*

*You whining marry-ed regretting your fate;*     **115**
*I dreamt you drowning, saved by your Mate!*

*You marriage factory three times around;*     **116**
*I dreamt you a mole, digging holes in the ground!*

*You hapless marry-ed with dreams of another;*     **117**
*I dreamt your wish granted,  t'was worse than the other.*

*You hapless marry-ed with more fish in the sea:*     **118**
*I dreamt you already hooked, your catch to be!*

*A pilgrim in progress to desperate to find;*     **119**
*I dreamt you already hooked, your catch to be!*

*You flaunting reprobate in house of gold;* **120**
*I dreamt you in a tent, to cover from the cold.*

*You sorrow(ed) pig harboring the pest of smite;* **121**
*I dreamt you devoured, by God's loving might.*

# FORWARD

The following poems, Reigntide, SwanDance, Overheard in the Gym, Magic Well and Sneakers after truth are a selection of works generated (INSPIRED) by my emergence into the spectacle and energy of sport at Anchor Bay High School spread over an eight year period. Many more poems and letters were created and submitted to the school and may be published under a separate title.

Abandoning sport in 1972, immediately following the Olympic trials, after being deluged by countless Out of Body Experiences suggesting to me (indeed intimating to me) there is more to life than sport, especially its competitive wiles to conquer the other. I was smitten by an inner drive to transform the outer discipline required of sport into inner discipline to transcend the passions of the body. Even to the point of considering going to a monastery. Being blessed to have come across the teachings of Gurdjieff and Ouspensky (see letter titled-To a young woman) I learned of the Fourth Way. The way of the Fakir; the Monk; the Yogi; then there is the way of the (FOURTH) namely, remain in the world but be not of it, takes even greater strength, indeed, a lifetime of "Work" on oneself under a profoundly specialized system of development from the usual sleep state to the waking state. The fourth way is esoteric ancient Orthodox (prebyzantine) Christianity. In short, original Christianity not watered down in consideration of man's inherent weakness to perfect himself!

After many years of study, and constantly seeing all outer events and images as metaphoric analogies of the inner terrain, I was blessed with good fortune to be, once again immersed into the experience of sport. This time, however, and thankfully so, as a mere spectator at Anchor Bay High School. The poems reveal my penchant for metaphors in sport as I look for ways God works to reveal Himself through athletic struggle. Afterall, Paul, the Apostle, says the spiritual life is akin to an athletic contest. Notice how various couplets intertwine to shed light on something internal as perforce the external forging.

Aside from the metaphors and union of inner with outer, these young athletes (male and female) are truly wonderful to watch. Salve for the soul they surely are! Athletics are a true foundation for spiritual growth; even life.

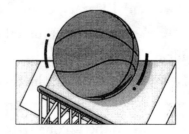

# Preface to Reigntide Poem

(Athletic Supremacy at a local High School)

Dear Coach and Varsity Basketball Team;

I was surely inspired to compose a poem (some sort of sequel to Ebbtide I guess you could call it) after watching your playmakes this past month. The victorious web you wove was indeed, a pleasure to witness. In short, I can only quip this:

| | |
|---|---|
| T | THRIVING |
| A | ATHLETES |
| R | REIGNED |
| S | SUPERB!! |

Sincerely yours,

Ron Gleason

I hope you enjoy the poem. I enjoy feeling it. I enjoy bringing words to life. I enjoy combining words to build images in the readers mind. WE ENJOY WATCHING YOUR NET-WORKING TO BUILD DEFENSE(S); TO BUILD ARTFUL OFFENDING ATTACKS; WE ENJOY YOUR SUCCESSES; OUR CHEERS GO OUT TO YOU IN

**Continued Preface to Reigntide Poem**

STILLNESS OF BODY; STILLNESS OF MIND; THAT'S THE
BRIDGE WE MUST BEAR; WE MUST CARVE TO UPHOLD THE
FORTUNE IN CENTEREDNESS; IN MEDITATIVE POSTURING
FOR THE UNEQUIVOCAL GEOMETRIC LAW IN THE UNSEEN
MATRIX WEAVE IS THAT PLUS(ES) ARE FOLLOWED BY
MINUS(ES) AND MINUS(ES) FOLLOWED BY PLUS(ES). THIS
PARODY PREVAILS TO FOSTER GROWTH AND IS
EXPERIENTIALLY VERIFIABLE AND GEE ARE ITS
WRENCHING OR EUPHORIC TENTACLES EVER PRESENT
AMID THE EBBTIDE OF SPORT!!!!!!!! NOW SOMEWHERE
DEEP WITHIN IS THAT MYSTIC CENTER; THAT PRECIOUS
PEARL; THAT PHILOSOPHER'S STONE; THAT GREAT
KINGDOM WITHIN!!! THE OUTER TRAVAIL OF SPORT IS A
WONDROUS TEACHER OF COSMIC GEOMETRICS FOR ITS
MARRIAGE WITH PARODY IS KEENLY FELT BY ALL OF US
WHO HAVE ENDURED THE PLEASURES AND WOES OF
ATHLETICS!

> May the blessings be,
> So mote it Be !

Somewhere hidden deep down from above
Lies a kernel, its lurking glove;                                    2

Fingers out stretched curdling its mold
Speaking its tongue in words of gold!                               4

This matrix weave yarned in silk
Is an *alchemist's dream; unspoiled milk.                           6

Transmute, transmute his special skill,
This to that, sorrow to thrill.                                     8

The lab his playpen to create anew;
Miracles pour from out of the blue.                                10

His secrets cryptic; his hopes no bend,
But believe believe is his only intend.                           12

FROM ** "TWELVE ANGRY MEN"
TO        " TWELVE HAPPY MEN"                                      14

Your matrix weave yarned in silk
Hoarded the basket the foes you bilk.                              16

FROM "TWELVE ANGRY MEN"
TO       "TWELVE HAPPY MEN"                                        18

* Alchemist: Turns baser metals into gold and seek to find a universal elixir of life using
either magical power or process of Transmuting. ** 12 Angry men was a term coined
by the coach to add fuel to their fire to win.

# REIGNTIDE

*Your lab boasted the hard court bounce ;*
*Your prey is foiled by a steadied pounce ! !*                    20

*The alchemist's metals his glory in gold;*
*Your glory to, but it can't be sold !*                    22

*TRANSMUTE TRANSMUTE Twelve Angry Men;*
*TRANSMUTE TRANSMUTE Twelve Happy Men*                    23

# REIGNTIDE

From this to that from hope to slope
You climbed and climbed back up the rope !                    26

Where lies the secret dawn of it all ?
So cryptic? It dangles inside the ball !                      28

You dance the bill and stemmed the tide;
This pearl inside the ball never lied.                        30

Look on the tip, the tip of your nose;
Look in the mirror, the reflection knows.                     32

Who is this man staring right back
In the glass? A man of knack;                                 34

A man with gleam and roar in his eyes
The forge of youth his vigor belies.                36

His game orchestrated like a clever sleuth
For those eighteen the world's his booth;                38

Practice makes perfect on the varnished court
But sculpting the PEARL you can't run short! !                40

Is this to be taken as Holy Letter?
Well now, look at these Un-holy letters;                42

By coincidence or preordain,
Look at their echo down the lane;                44

E : E N T H U S I A S M *
B : B R I L L I A N T L Y
B : B R I D L I N G
T : T H E
I : I N V A D E R S
D : D A R I N G
E : E N H A N C E M E N T                51

Except those twelve, "Twelve Angry Men:"
Their matrix weave their gold in the den.                62

* Ebbtide is a title of poem submitted earlier in season.

NOW! these twelve, "Twelve Happy Men,"
Are richer inside; Oh silken pen!                    64

The offenders attack your prickly branch
But cower to your flowering avalanche.              66

Erewhile your churning anvil of might
altered the charts out of sight.                     68

Ambers aflame hobbling the trotter
Cuz the alchemy you borne was hotter!              70

Now  ambers of fate firing your souls
Added hone to skills chalking your goals,           72

Linking the web of cohesion's chain
Like milk to butter; like clouds to rain;           74

One link here; one link there,
Ah! the music is in the air! !                       76

Your footwork gallop taunts and impales;
Clankity clank the enemy fails                       78

Again and again; your gold's in the stove;
You redressed the mark and INTERWOVE! !            80

In the cauldron of your Varsity plight
You cooked a seed that'll live forthnight,          82

A baker's DOZEN or a coach's dream;
Academics your slate his high esteem;                    84

Yet you spoke, you spoke your piece
Maneuvering a globe with artful release.                86

A STONED PHILOSOPHER OR A PHILOSOPHER'S STONE? 88
A DANCE OF WORDS OR ACTIONS TO THE BONE?
ALL FANS BY YOUR SIDE WERE INDELIBLY SHOWN
INCITE THOSE BAYERS AND YOU'LL MAKE them GROAN! 90

A rage to live or a rage to win,
You made them moan and sulk their chin!                 92

AT HOME OR AWAY YOU PRINT YOUR FLAIR;
TWELVE HAPPY MEN, THEY MET YOUR STARE!                  94

AT HOME OR  AWAY NO DOWSING YOUR FLAIR;
TWELVE HAPPY MEN, NO CLIMBING YOUR STAIR!               96

A scented trail you smelled the rose,
BELIEVE BELIEVE you rightfully chose!                   98

A hearty youth or youths with a heart,
They couldn't quell your grit from start!              100

Frolic and mirth your due celebrate;
Court finesse your sole inebriate;                     102

A wage you learned from study and play;
Indeed your fortune that can't decay! 104

A timely herald for a senior's swan song
Or a timely herald for a junior's head long. 106

Somewhere hidden deep down from above
Lies a kernel its lurking glove. 108

As far above, So far below;
The globe handlers of the court
Danced a step none could distort;
The alchemist's dream is your bestow! ! 112

FROM "TWELVE ANGRY MEN"
TO    "TWELVE HAPPY MEN" 114

Transmut(ed) Your nectar fruit;
Recoil soul and listen to the FLUTE! 116

A bird with WINGS or an angel that SINGS;
He's hidden from SIGHT cause humans FRIGHT.
THE EYE OF *SINGLE with that he'll MINGLE
He is the LIGHT all mighty MIGHT!!! 120

Look deep down for the philosopher's Stone;
The clue's in your game the discipline you hone; 122

A pearl beyond price its weight is none;
His yoke is easy; He is the Son! 124

"TWELVE HAPPY MEN"
LET DOWN YOUR DUKE!
"TWELVE HAPPY MEN"
YOU BRIDLED THE FLUKE! 130

"TWELVE HAPPY MEN"
YOU REIGNED THE TIDE! ! 132

---

\* Single eye is inner eye that upon opening views a refulgent light. Certain methods are needed to open this third eye.

The clue's in your game the discipline you hone.

# SWANDANCE

*(Those Glorious Pom Pon Girls at a local HighSchool)*

GEE those sky dancers are a sight;
A sight to remember; they paint their space
With the ease of swans in flight.

Whatever their rank; whatever their flank
Let them inspire SWISH SWISH, SWISH SWISH,
A rebound draw and CLANKITY CLANK ! !

Just look at those perfect temples of clay
Sculpted from the manna of an untiring Hand,
Swim underwater while on the deck at bay.

Is not the TARgantuan gym one huge
Ship on a cruise toppling waves
That needn't leave shore for refuge?!

So short, it seems, the swan's perform
Their leaps, their chants and undulations
But time is stopped by absorption in a gaze
That cowers to the moment; its jubilations,
Carving in air echoes of each others' phase.
A vortex borne bubbles on their platform!!!

## SWANDANCE

As your eyes glisten through the tapestry you weave;
As the aura of its space remains after you leave;
As your fluidity's flow filters space for all to conceive;
As your geometry of lines zero gravity by artistry you achieve;
As you trace arms of each others' form your sleeve becomes her
sleeve;
As you write your script on stage without floor with no pens to
heave;
As your sculpted forms brush the canvas for others to believe;
As your forms meld to one like grapes to wine; like water to jello,
Miming the cadence of melodies you perceive;


### AND FINALLY


As you brush the canvas, you become the canvas;
As you zero gravity, you become gravity;
As you trace a line, you become the line;
As you create an aura, you become its shadow;
As you write your script, you become the pen;
As your fluidity streams, your language becomes fluent;
As your space empties, your windprint is left in the air;
As your bodies sing, a song is heard without ears;
As your eyes glisten, their beam lights a wick;
FOR SELF JOY AND GAIETY ARE THE MESSAGE THEY PAINT!!!


### I GIVE UP!!

No words can scroll the images you course; you mime in space;
But the euphoria felt by those moments you captured in space
Is ferried yonder erasing its trace hastening a sense;

# SWANDANCE

A longing for a repeat performance.
Any buoy s left on the waters of the mind are lifted
To make room for the Swans of the Lake ! ! !
Wadingly your,
Waiting for more,

And now do you see what really is missed, you orchestrators
Of the court ere heeding conductor's words to stop infiltration!

A half time course chart
Or a half time space dart! ! !

May the blessings stay
For those ANCHORS on the BAY ! ! !

Thankfully Yours,

Ron Gleason


S; S I M P L Y
W; W O N D E R F U L
A; A N O T H E R
N; N O T C H
D; D O N N E D
A; A M A Z I N G
N; N O N E
C; C O U L D
E; E X P L A I N

# Overheard In The Gym

(Imaginary conversation between a basketball, backboard, floor and players)

Mr. Ball says to Miss Rim, "Why are you so small?" Miss Rim retorts, "Why are you so big, heavy and hard; I have feelings too you know? "Mr. Ball responds, "What about me, all those fingers soiling my coat and bouncing my brains out!" "Yeh, I see what you mean but then I didn't know you had any brains, Mr. Ball, "quips Miss Rim. Miss Rim further declared, "What about all those touchy fingers tinkering with my rope woven skirt, especially those slam dunks, they drive me up a backboard! "Mr. Ball responds, " If I had brains you Miss's wouldn't have anything to complain about!" " Enough! Enough! with such self centered converse, " says Mr. Backboard. " Without me," states Mr. Backboard, " You babblers wouldn't even be able to play games with each other. I support Miss Rim and I absorb all those Ball bangs off my spine; it drives me to the shakes and I ponder, why did I ever ask God for this thankless, burdensome job. I must have been an Overpaid athlete in a past life to deserve all this...!" Mother Floor, overhearing all this complaining rubble, retorts, "Look at me, I had to die A Saint to earn this reward as an athlete's trampoline; My poverty is your support; Your dirt is my inhale; Your thumps are my caress; Your verbiage is my music; Your glee is my food; Your sadness is my laundry; No, God has not forsaken me, after all, he sees to it my emotional vessel is on eternal flush making it clear as a whistle, else, how could I handle all these ebbs of youth at sport! You see, Mr. Backboard, you are the backbone of Sport, but all these young spirits are the backbone of Life! If you keep complaining, Mr. Backboard, I'm gonna ask God that He cause you to be reborn a Donkey." "Okay, Mother Floor, says Mr. Backboard," I get the message, but tell me, Mother Floor, why has God allowed our Bay Men to lose seven straight games when skills displayed seemed equal.

"Mother Floor responds, "FEAR NOT, my child, if God hasn't forsaken me, a mere floor, how could HE forsake HIS Ebullient Youth. You see Mr. Backboard, God knows His Bay children are so fortified that He thought they were ready for the next step on the ladder of life, namely, to reward them with sorrow; He works in strange ways, afterall. This way, introspection is fostered and blessings are counted. You see, my child, disappointment cracks open the heart, and a Heart never opened can't receive HIS LOVE! "After lending all this wisdom to eavesdroppers in the gym, Mr. Ball, and Miss Rim, Mother Floor Further states, "Besides, God Chooses not to downturn the elated spirits of teams entering the Bastion of Anchor Bay's Court of Dreams!" "Mr. Backboard seems satisfied with Her response and returns to his meditative trance readied to absorb those pitiless Ball bangs. Meanwhile, Mr. Ball and Miss Rim murmur a soliloquy as they reposition themselves prepped for the main event; It goes, "All that sifting through the swamp land of mind; ?All those self pitying complaints sowing inertia are all for naught; and as God Disposes, mortals dream of proposing. How does Mother Floor know all this stuff, anyway? "God hears and whispers, "I made Mother Floor the Tree of Life, afterall, where do you think all that comely wood came from?!

What did the Metaphorster say to the punster? "Get outa my path, I'm trying to kick a field goal!" What say the Punster to the Metaphorster: "you broke my finger off with your foot, you brute, now how can I point the way to truth you guzzling dullard!? God intercedes, hearing all this gobblety babble; Fret not my children, stifle your tongues and pay attention to the game, and SAVE the muck in your mental swamp for the Nut House Doctor!

Sincerely,
Ronne Gleason

# Sneakers After Truth!
### (How a simple softball game vouchsafes a metaphor for truth)

The following is a copy of a meditation draft I presented to the 1989 Varsity Softball team. I hope you enjoy it.

SOME TIDDIE BIDDIES
TO CHEW ON
*******************

A SELF HYPNOTIC
MEDITATION CARD FOR SNEAKERS AFTER TRUTH
I N   S P O R T
I.E.
HOW TO STEAL HOME PLATE THE SLY WOMAN'S
WAY AND LIVE TO TELL THE TRUTH;
SEE COACH I TOLD YOU I CAN DO;
WE ARE NOW ONE RUN CLOSER TO VICTORY!

Swing and sing your way to first;
Glance, then dance your way to second;
Sway, then pray your way to third;
AND THEN, RUN YOUR BUNS ON HOME!!!

[MAY THE BASES BE]     [MAY THE BLESSINGS BE]

And who ever said a metaphor espousing a Divine Truth could not be contained within sport!?

**OBSERVE:**

Initial effort to bring the human body (machine) out of deep sleep (step into batters box to take first swing) then upon contact with ball, [SING] (out of joy for making contact) your way to first base and experiencing the benevolence of the blessing for taking the first step as a seeker after truth (Know Thyself!) After a period of jollity and mirth, you take another peek, this time, even deeper down into the inner abyss (GLANCE) then, once the decision is made, you come out of the deepened meditative trance and [DANCE] your way to second base, knowing all is well to do so, as the impulses are growing further from the worldly senses and closer to the Sacred Impulse, hence the ease and confidence to dance your way to the second step in VOLUNTARIZING, YOUR OWN EVOLUTION; WEAVING YOUR DESTINY WITH MASTERY. T E E T E R I N G [SWAY] on second base as you are beginning to sense, with an ethereal sensibility, that the further you climb the ever so high mountain of Truth Within ere greater the danger, hence the caution, i.e. the SWAY! A rarified intuitive feeling at this point inspires in one a necessity to [PRAY] and lo, this guiding light to pray adds momentum to your temple (move faster) blessing you with the capture; a third base steal. Jubilant over your new found success (awareness) through SINGING, GLANCING, SWAYING AND PRAYING while OBSERVING the central most force on the ball diamond (pitcher or demon) who seeks to get you off the Base Path (knock you off your journey back home to God) you become tentative in your glorious plight to steal HOME PLATE and recapture your Divine heritage i.e the point from which you commenced your journey as an eager player succeeding in making a base hit. Wallowing in this tentativeness for only a short time, YOU CONCLUDE THIS LUKEWARMNESS IN MY LAST STEP TO REACH HOME BASE is ludicrous, unfounded and cowardly, CONCLUSION arrived at by the eager player (seeker) sends out the spirited vibrations to the Far Country (Higher Worlds) and magic occurs as the GUARDIAN ANGEL PROVOKES IN THE COACH TO UTTER ALOUD, "GO FOR IT YOUNG BASE STEALER (Hungry Seeker) you've demonstrated the courage to get this far (third base) the final step is now yours in God!" Double magic occurred in this last step to steal home. The guardian angel of the ardent seeker after truth (original home base) caused the catcher to miss the ball! The Absolute is no respecter of persons (equal terrain for all.) Aware of the risk factor, you went for it; you ran your BUNS on HOME! The HOMESTEAD REGAINED, ALAS! The magical base stealer quips to her coach, "SEE coach, I told you I CAN DO; my efforts, gaiety, slyness and courage paid off." Bemused by the remarks of his young ball player, the coach retorts, "Don't forget who your guardian angel was during your hesitation to go all the way; I coaxed you,

REMEMBER!" 'Satisfied, the young player (seeker) bows in reverence to this Coach (Angel) murmuring to herself, "Is it really true their are special agents of God and distributors of His Spirit Force to intervene in worldly affairs that reside in the FAR COUNTRY exclusively for my Benefit? "I know so," she secretly senses, then Utters aloud, "THANKS COACH FOR LETTING ME STAND IN THE BATTERS BOX THAT SIGNALLED THE BEGINNING OF A BRAND NEW LIFE; A BRAND NEW LIFE THAT ENABLES ME TO SCULPT TO HEART'S CONTENT A SIMPLY AWESOME LANDSCAPE BEGGING CREATION FROM THE INNER CHAMBER OF MY BEING; THAT EXOTIC PEARL BEYOND PRICE!"

**************************************************

*end of copy/meditation draft submitted to 1989
Varsity Softball Team...

Human interest: Baseball boasts a mystical heritage going back to ancient times. Though not within the scope of this paper to elaborate, the selection of the numbers, three and nine, were a result of the ancient followers acknowledged wisdom in the numbers three and nine as extracted by the Enneagram. The Enneagram is presently used in Universities around the world for personality typing. The enneagram is a major force in Esoteric Orthodox Christianity.

Forward

Magic Well

I was Inspired to create this metaphor of the Magic Well as I was witness to your ceaseless drive to excel, especially, being victorious on the scoreboard in three of your last four games. You kept digging, digging and digging, in what appeared an endless dry- - - score spell. You never accepted the possibility that the well would come up dry in spite of your enthusiastic efforts to excel. Though you rang the scoreboard to your favor the last three of four games spelling your victory, (even if the scoreboard suggested scores, out of favor), your relentless vigor and mature spirit during the digging of your well; during the digging inside or outside for net swishes, bespeaks a victory no matter what the numbers read!

You gushed the soil with an exhilarating harvest bringing joy and excitement to dehydrating peers and fans longing for the water well of victory. You watered their souls with your dance; With your orchestrated plays and Faith! (The last game was a Classic, Guys!)

Hidden deep within you must of been a taste of Salt-ed Water to motor your turnaround. That salt water had magic in it, in spite of a victory drought, that found you, so close, so many times, to achieving higher scores, than your opponent. Wafting through this mysterious maze of near victories so frequently prior to the third quarter of season, that is, I pondered, can their spirits continue to ride on the wind of steadfastness? One pointedness and exuberance? (That you Did!)

And how about those high pitched voices piping through the ether, echoing musical tunes from a celestial womb! And how about those twirling script writers tracing notes in space?!

Their dancing flare chisels in space
Imprints that marble murals,
No art museum could compete with!

Is woman, through her grace and softened might, that hidden motor inside the mack truck called man. Man carries so many burdens playing the worldly chess game; could woman be his secret propeller hidden beneath the hood of his mack-truck like body and spirit?! He gets the name while she fuels his spirit!?

Their frolic and penchant for mirth,
Suggests they're a plant from God,
Nestled in stone to extract all cares!

Their beauty and finely sculpted bodies,
Tenders the senses to virgin heights;
They're a diamond in the wind; untouchable! untouchable!

Caption

Dear Coach and Varsity Basketball Team;

Please find enclosed a poem that I was inspired to write. It's a metaphorical poem  especially characteristic of the comeback the guys made during the last quarter of the season. The last game was a trigger creating in me certain images that I felt compelled to put on paper. I hope you enjoy it. The pulse of the poem commemorates the flow of the season.

Sincerely Yours,

Ronne  Gleason

# The Magic Well
(Survival & Character Of LocalHigh School Basketball Team)

Their is this story of a little boy,
His mother and two year old baby,
And their barren well!
This well has been dry for seven months!
A hankering crept into the mother,
"Go fetch some water from our dry well, son,
I have this good feeling
God can see your baby sister wilting away
FROM DEHYDRATION!"
Yonder the boy goes, zestfully
Heeding the call of his hopeful mother.
Now at the well crest,
He yanks and yanks hoping for a miracle,
Water that is;
One pull, tow pulls, three pulls-four,
Dry , dry and ever so dry,
Dust even sails as bucket flails the crock.
Harried by his futile attempts to draw water
And honor his mommy's expectations,
And bring relief to his baby sister,
Tears trickled down this little boy's cheeks
Filtering into his mouth
Greeting his tongue with a taste of salt.
He remembers hearing in Sunday School,
Jesus "IS THE SALT OF THE EARTH."
Pondering and pondering mommy's are never wrong,

She would not have sent me YONDER
To our seven months Dry Well
Unless a spirited voice moved her to do so.
Putting two and two together:
The symbolic taste of salt on his tongue
And mommy's are always right,
He became overwrought with inspiration;
And mustering these tiny symbolic SEEDS
OF FAITH WITH NO BUDS,
He jumped into the well like a dove without wings
To see if, indeed, the well bottom had even a smidgen
Of Moisture.
Dry, dry, dry to the bone he learned.
Not accepting this fact,
He uplifted himself to ground level and fetched a shovel amid his
private soliloquy:
This is my chance to prove to mommy
I can take over where PaPa left off when he died
Digging in a coal mine; I will bring life
To this family DIGGING for water;
The water of Life!
Returning to the barren well he hailed his grit
In single mind mode focussed to conquer
Dust unto dust, water unto water,
AND DUST TO WATER!
A marriage in hell or a marriage in heaven;
Pregnant with hope,
Divorced from doubt,
In durst defiance to accept defeat,

This little boy grafted his own proverb;
"If a dried out seed can sprout a tree;
A Tree of Life,
Then a dried out dust particle
Can sprout a water molecule;
For if He is the dry Salt Of Earth,
And mommy is the WELL SPRING that gave me life,
This heavenly union
Can do naught but anoint my efforts to succeed!"
With these ponderings in hand,
And shovel clasped by his tightening grip,
He commenced his DIG; he digs and digs and digs,
Filling bucket after bucket with dried out dirt;
Hoisting and hoisting, to seeming no end,
Each barren bucket to ground level
But to no avail; To no avail.
This little ten your old boy,
With the faith of a mustard seed,
Was building muscles only boasted by a weightlifter.
Unceasing in his secret prayer:
(A soliloquy of a blooming heart)
"Mommy's are always right,
And Jesus is my Salt; my life giver out of dust,"
He forged ahead his enormous task,
Albeit the odds of finding water shrank with time.
After two days of constant digging,
He was sinking further and further
Into the bowel of the earth.

Not even taking time to gulp some food.
Tiring alas, he retired his shovel,
And sat down eyes closing,
As he leaned against the well wall,
He falls asleep.
Dreams and visions greeted him kindly,
As he earned his right to snooze,
And wander away from the cares of the world
Into realms beyond the gravity of earth!
Encountering visual splendors of the *aerial plane,
He witnessed an elephant bathing in a river,
Drawing water up into his trunk,
And showering it over his body.
Strangely, after being completely clean,
He digs into the river bottom,
Sucks up some mud with his trunk
And showers his body with it.
After cleaning so carefully with water,
He covers his body with mud once again.
Only then is he satisfied that his bath is finished,
Imagined the little boy during his dream.
Ever roaming about the ethereal planes,
Awed by the panoramic terrain,
He encounters two angels
Who guide him to the third heaven.

---

* First plane encountered after death; Out of body journey or dream. One is besieged by an array of disembodied spirits whose sole intent is to tempt one into a variety of self directed vices. This is a plane of profound hazard but we must all pass through it.

He is greeted by his PaPa,
All clad in white robe,
And twenty years younger in *appearance,
Who, on authority of God, is now a spirit guide.
"My son," exhorts the spirit guide,
"I'm the one who planted that urge in your mother
To cause you to fetch some water in the dry well.
I'm the one who planted that urge in you to succeed
At all costs.
I even caused you to witness a bathing elephant
To teach you, by example, how NOT to succeed.
You see, my son, earthlings,
Imagining they're focused,
Clean away stifling distractions
From the body of their mind,
Only to, in short time,
Rub the Mud of distracting desires,
Totally unrelated to objective at hand,
All over the body of the mind!
On and on it goes;
The mind becomes one's swampland!
Because, my son, I already know the future,
(God has graced me with this special knowledge)
I felt I'd intervene and encourage your efforts
That are, presently, one pointed and focused,
And caution you against human tendency,
Namely, to avoid the trappings
OF THE ELEPHANT MIND SET!
Bless you my son, YOU WILL REACH WATER!

*Virtuous departed souls take on the physical appearance they once had during their youthful middle years; A simple reward for living a good, virtuous life!

And I pray that when you die and translate to my plane,
God will make you into a spirit guide like me!"
Returning to his body, the little boy,
Thoroughly rested and besieged
By an even greater desire to accomplish his task
As he basks in the glorious promptings
Of his immortalized, sainted PaPa,
Commences his well digging once again.
Not long in to his renewed energy surge,
He not only found moistened dirt,
He punctured through a bowel,
A bowel leading to an underground stream
That welcomed the sharpened spade
With a water gush go prodigious
It hoisted the little boy
To well top and beyond its crest,
Flooding the nearby terrain with WATER!
A literal fountain, water toppling to mist.
Being hugged to life by the well wisher,
Tears of joy puddled this little boy's face,
Caressing his lips with the taste of Salt
Igniting a recall of his secret prayer,
And his other world experience.
"Finally", He quipped to himself,
"Mommy and my baby sister will get water;
And Wow! wait 'til I tell them
Of my experience meeting PaPa in heaven!"
Sharing this good news with his family,
Mommy voiced her response to her euphoric son:
"I ALWAYS KNEW THAT WELL HAD MAGIC IN IT!"

# A CHILD IS BORN
## JUNE 1971
### (Author's quest to conquer base passions early in life)

My unyielding earth-born toil begins,
Provoking sumptuous upheavels of whims,

As I mal-adroitly roam and traverse,
Forever teaming the boundless universe.

Meandering over the taunting terrain,
Wayward and aimless I scathe in vain,

Sighting a shadow and off I travail
Along nature's shackling and frolicsome trail

Unable to find the insatiable orgasms
Forever titillating, yet turning to sarcasm.

OH! how I churned, forever forced
To kneel to mirages endlessly endorsed.

Woe unto me, they seemed so real
I screamed to the heaven's my carnal appeal;

But spirit so deadening from cravings base,
I beseeched release from my carnal chase.

Spirits dampened, and face filling with blotches
While counting binding and vexing notches

Of nature's mounting unkindly ways,
I saw saneness threatened in coming days.


Debauchery now ingrained in nature's tide,
Welcome's darkness's descending ride.


Virtue and austerity now left abyss;
Earthly joys unsated serving as bliss;


Wails of woe emerge from deep
Mourning the folly of my carnal treat.


Seeing the eternal orgasm beyond attaining,
And joys of present no longer sustaining,


Melancholy sweeps me far asunder
Where I hastily await salve for blunder.


Feeling like an aimless ridden libertine
Woefully in need of early pristine,


Many times I imagined blooming in health,
Swallowing sun-rays, reaping heavenly wealth,


While sowing and harvesting fruits of the sod
Like an unwaried leaping arthropod.


Thirsting to be on ships asail,
I eagerly prepared, but to no avail.

In forbearing beguilement, but helpless in spite,
My vessels enlarged, begging respite.

As lights of darkness deceived my sight,
Offering  mirages to soothe my plight,

Like starving buzzards carousing a corpse
Ensnare earthly waters of all sorts,

Illusive earthly slime ambushed
My unpured mind so slyly pushed,

Causing me to raise unsavory questions
Like who wants redeeming or like suggestions.

Turbid-bred feelings of ennui grew,
And joys unquenched followed me into

The tranquil darkness of night late
Alone with gusting winds opiate,

Where pondering's submerge in solemn meditation,
Bid thoughts prolific recapping negation.

No longer forlorn and bereft of hope,
I captured a newly envisioned scope.

Intuiting my frailties, I sensed a mar,
And sought knowledge like a sinking day-star.

Preferring more quiet to cohabitude,
I lessened carnality, tasting a new mood,

And retired into hidden regions of the mind,
Discovering arcane cumbrous to unwind.

In my intellectual plight, I showed erudition,
But undigested theorems vexed my condition.

Concern for scurrying metaphors
Raised many questions the commoner abhors,

But as debauchery seemingly burned away,
Other passions rising from ashes layed-away,

Because desires stomached in wantoness vanish
Like air-born vapors rise and banish.

Still fettered, I wandered to the wondrous lake-shore,
And dolefully yelped in a violent uproar,

Confessing, "Theorems make me sedate,
But leave me dimensions from primordial's state."

Perennial passions I attested to be,
I ardently sought a higher decree.

I hoped by way of food levelling
To ward off further bedevilling.

The nectareous herbs of the tree prevailed,
Expelling meats for spiritual feelings were haled

Ever constantly and moderation
Was a frenzied and endless discoloration.

A food decrease, while opening gateways
For long-buried rejuvenating cosmic rays

That license hard sought, but flourishing contentment,
Caused reviving empyrean inhabitants

To praise my purgatorial doomed debate
As I yearned the omnipotent to emulate.

Un-harnessed from terror rising events I became,
As heavenly praise I received, for fate's game

Looking headlong to broad-loomed skies I stood
First speechless, then melting into tears of brotherhood,

I spoke, "Oh fairing Creator, how I thank Thee,
Creator wise, and your Divine decree,

For allowing nature's tumultuous grind
To rise above fate's unkind."

Embraced by fervor, I purported recomfort
From daunt severe, but thoughts revert

From gratitude and turn to another
Indwelling urge as ecstasies fluttered,

Knawed dark chambers of my heart's abyss,
Recoiling a need fated amiss.

Long-hearing empty voice that caused apparent
Puzzling enigmas added impairment,

Expounded long periods of silence for a choice
As I tired of crabbed and empty voice.

All this I did, thinking very near
I've come to Divinity's secret sphere.

Zeal quieted while adoring the forest's prow,
Beseemed me bid laurels to rest for now.

Erewhile, my inner voice suddenly spoke
A fruit precious as new love's yoke.

What happened to love, a most savoring task;
Have you taken off your barren mask?"

"Sure," stammered I, "I was in love,
But it thwarted my urge to soar like a dove."

"That was not love, "rebuked my inner voice,
"It was onanism, so masked by rejoice

Over carnal phantasms from painted hussies,
You yielded profusely, overlonely to be fussy.

Wiser you be from sensuous affairs,
But staunch you'll be revering barren snares"

Time is lapsing in my internal flight,
But love deprived, extoling smite,

Acts as a scavenger upon my new-born
Sight, provoking my soul to mourn.

Upon rising with the sun's comforting rays one day,
I strolled out by wondrous waters and lay.

During the sepulcher of thought a yearn
For love reached its peak discern.

Bewailed, I felt a falling leave,
Wavering in the wind, barred from reprieve,

Hopelessly lost in the wallow of despondency,
With incurable yearnings for love's correspondency.

"Oh Divinity," I cried, as I tearfully eyed The heavens, "how can
Such awesome tensions arise?"

A message from celestial spheres echoed down,
Breathingl, "Oh pleading mortal, your clowning

Mourned the heavens all while you tried
Because Jesus Christ you not only defied,

But closed the door on His all consuming Will
Becoming to your own will a slave for thrill."

"You mean," responded I to the angelic sound,
"That sacrifice contained in wisdom profound

That's unstained by wreaks of vanity
Is willed not by me, but by God through me?"

"Yes," hummed the angelic voice as it returned
To its source where it lull's in taciturn.

Conversion near, could the Lord be in range?
Then erelong I espoused an unexpected change:

Thirst unquenched for knowledge abstract
You can have Sir Wisdom to keep in tact;

Joys of earth you can rent to distort
Sir Passion; Just leave your feeble resort

For self of old, for betwixt the two,
Arrest the frail and choose the new.

The way of Christ I mean; His path
So straight it frees me from debates of wrath;

His burden so light, it does well spurn me
From a tame untrimmed I longed to be.


Stricken with wonder, I feel suddenly pinned
While faced by terrifying on-rushing winds.*


Kindled by the succour of emptiness, I melt
While <u>leaping</u> from my body where long-time dwelt,**


As winds of ecstasy swallow the spark
That burns with heaven to re-embark,


And hurls my now loosed soul into spheres
Where visions beautific sublimely appear.


Most electrifying though, while wandering around
The cosmic plains was a hallowing sound


Resounding, "Jesus is coming," that nursed
My faith in untimely bible verse


So far beyond fathom of humans minds
I scorned my attachment to earthly grind.


I thought the following verse upon returning
From heavenly portals unblemished discerning's:


"Pleasures fleeting, soaring all heights,
But tasteless to my soul is its delights

* Sounds that preceded out of body journey. ** Actual exiting from physical body.

For they belabor flights from my body below,
And waylay melodies flickered from cosmos

That inform naught is below but emotions
Feigned for want of consoling potions;

Memories appeased by pleasures of old;
Senses blinded by images that unfold;

Knowledge acquired for quarrels unholy;
Opinions intoxicated by appetites solely;

Intellectuals calloused, framed for show;
Theories applauded, then brought to woe;

Wisdom of earth so crafty it leads
One's soul to where the devil breeds;

And faith unwanting for fear of darkness,
And repenting tears lamenting past starkness."

Oh! secret darkness of faith, your cloud
So dark and dressed in mystery shroud,

Sends my repose, undulled by earth's
Crafty light and countless deluding mirth's,

Into rapture's where I await the final gale
From God to clasp me in His next inhale.

Bewildered by changes overwrougting my soul,
I melted into despair begging a new goal.


Tears a- fount and burning puddled my face
As I pondered my heresy and its disgrace.


Oh my God, I am enraptured;
Knees now weakening, I feel captured.


Humiliated and dumbfounded, confess I must,
Before I return to barren dust.


Here is my song, Oh Lord so dear,
I hoped you've waited so long to hear:


"Fallen to my knees I now to stay
For reasons no other than to pray."


Oh Lord, please hear my long forgotten plea,
And protect me against the devil's glee.


Wretched my ways, sordid my cares,
Only because I caress the devil's snares.


Pleasures I indulge to forge jubilee,
Caring not I'm of the fallen spree.


Open to cloy pleasures of earth,
Forgive me Lord for jollity in mirth.

How feeble to revere the painted dame,
I now acknowledge her tampered frame.

Much to my distress I sought her in vain,
Forgetting bless-ed Mary was pure and plain.

But then I found what I deserved
By ignoring the example Jesus preserved.

My only retort is now to change
Ways of old and narrow the range.

Sex-ruled lady, unworthy to have
For she sells herself as a mask for salve.

Man-hunting she goes, slyly campaigning,
Hoping for lay's or anything but abstaining.

Mortal I am, but regenerate I must,
Oh Lord, destroy my self-born lust.

All foods I thought so proper to crave,
Heedless me, for I didn't behave.

Distempered and listless as a bloated dyspeptic,
Backwards I slid like a puffed-up skeptic,

For the diet of Genesis of herbs and fruit
I sluffed; Heedlessness thence took root.

Timeworn wastes my stomach long-saves,
And exhaustingly greets peristaltic waves.

Aghast by hunger I vomit and bluster,
Attempting to be a foreign food adjuster.*

Food deposits hardening, defecating much less,**
Waste building up help constipation progress.

Seminal vesicles now crushed by my bulging bladder***
A release I need, hence my sexual chatter.

Intercourse I meet, air-borning my sperm;
So joyed, it increased my sexual yearn.

Relief I found, but at the Lord's expense,
For the fluid contained His life essence.

How natural emissions were made to seem,
Oh Lord, I destroyed you in the earth-born stream.

Menstruation, intercourse the same,
For Jesus is plucked[up during the game.

Lamenting my actions, I sneered all ladies;
And they dumbfounded by my strangeness displayed,

Whetted my thirst to welcome their bribe;
Oh Lord, I beseech you, what do you prescribe?

*Foods not of the trees.**Cooked foods are constipating. *** Seminal vesicles are irritated by protein foods like meat etc. & other cooked foods do increase sexual desire by causing pressure in genital area.

"Your lady tells you you're quite strange,
And yet, was not Adam utterly estranged

To Eve when she was deceived by the coiled
Serpent while Adam was not despoiled?"

Erewhile, Eve said to Adam, "Come follow Me;"
Deception Adam did swallow

By consenting to a whim meant to entrap,
And offer chastity a chance to unwrap.

So lost he became in her opening dark,
He mocked not joys of his sexual embark.

Yet wishing release from the slippery cave,
She closed her legs on the earthly grave

To keep intact her mislead man
Who ever deny's the cosmic plan

Its chance to lift him up from desires
Base where rest in my Father aspires.

Him looking through a glass quite darkly she knows
Deep down; she flees from her weakly beau's,

Becoming weary of her captive's carnal ways,
Wanting another who hasn't gone astray,

Because the spark of God within her
Wants the man who's strong and pure

So she can have the strength to conquer
The serpent that lies ever-coiling within her.

Alas she finds her saintly man,
And stems the torrent of the beastly clan.

Forsaking men so easy to capture
She now beholds her saint's enrapture,

And lives in the always present Glory
Of God where carnal acts quite boring

Fade asunder and orgiastic activity
Is not desired because they become the activity

Themselves, forever unfolding amidst
The eternal orgasm's encircling bliss."

Thus saith the Lord, as I do imagine,
So enlivening to know, I relished holy discipline.

Regenerated woman, when are you to be found?
Oh yes, when I'm purified beyond earthly-bound!

Effrontery I thought I must aspire;
I pawned my soul for sake of hire

While thoughts entertained by excess money
Stemmed from wants of a classy honey,

Forgetting a farmer is content at least
Because he doesn't attract a plastic beast.

So long it took me to learn this truth,
I was nearly destroyed in my youth.

Mistresses, mistresses, I learned to enjoy,
But now the Lord I best employ.

My worldly retreat is not for spite,
But instead a thirst to unite

With my brethren, unmask a love I feigned,
And rest in the bosom of love regained.

Soil made fertile, greenery made blooming
Towers all types of worldly grooming.

Encountering's of the world, dangerous indeed,
Safer, is the invading insect breed

That ransacks my ripening orchard fruit,
For betrayal to my soul they can't impute.

False humility leads me on,
Yet better than being a worldly con.

Exalted by thoughts of monastic life,
I best await and tackle more strife

Else my body would take up space
As my spirit craved human race.

Although this childish fun is waning,
I beg the Lord strength for refraining.

Oh, the spurious savor of laughter and joy,
Grant me neither, for it meets with coy.

So blinded by want of knowledge to grasp,
I was prey to foibles of a shameless bombast

Infected by reasoning's merely human,
I worshipped false-prophets tirelessly assumin;

And calmness derived from the learned flock
Augmented my blindness to the hypnotic shock.

Relishing mystique of magical art,
Fear of the Lord overtook my heart.

For this, I thank the Lord I'm sure,
Else I'd be trapped by the devil's lure.

Garment of heretic I long-time worn,
Rudely omitting the virtue to mourn,

For envy of converts overtook my compassion
To surrender to anything but barren intellection.


Forming and reforming timeless time,
I loosed my reign on heavenly shrine


By praising my clarity of human perception,
Ignoring my own stout-hearted deception.


Opinions vainly acquired, then worn to decrepit,
The Lord knows I naught but increased my debit.


Forgive my heart its taint by pride
Of intellect; I grieve for I know I lied.


Trials numbered many, endless errors confuted,
In the eyes of the Lord, I'm still ill-refuted.


Wretched I am, oh says you too,
I'm plenteous worse than you'll ever view,


Because if you knew me half as well
As I know me you'd vomit and swell,


And swear I was an orphan from hell
Trumpeting poesy under a spell.


Relishing my strength, the Lord made me weak
Strength I had not to remain humbly meek;

For I had vile for vengeance to wreak,
Dear Lord, how could I dare bespeak.

Obsessed by rank and a gloated chide,
I scolded my brethren, misplacing my pride.

For a long-time past I layed the blame,
On them that honored not my name.

When urges vain led me astray,
I billed the bystander for my dismay,

And neglected my need to praise the Lord,
And wave good riddance to master Hoard.

Honors a few I have earned,
Oh Lord, untie self praise returned.

So often pomposity saturates my lust,
And lashes into fury my flaunting august.

Damn my wretched yearn for fame,
Dear Lord, your mercy I forgot the same.

I bade my pride daring to swell
By feasting on flattery's soothing spell.

Benefitting from rebukes appearing callous,
Save me responding(s) swelled by malice,

Else I'll destroy my hopes of redemption
By injuring my brethren's rightly intention.

Swept from true basis, borning begrudge,
I crippled my soul playing the judge.

Judging the source, avoiding its worth,
My brethren's reproof, I pray rebirth.

Wearied by talks of stale remarks,
I now prefer more private embarks.

The wise and unwise serve as my teacher,
Oh Lord, I mean not to be a leecher.

My brethren I rebuke so I can learn,
Hoping to provoke reproof's in return.

Countless customs I have now learned;
Hope not to late to unmold the burn;

Nowise, I'd be a puppet of fate
Weeping and sighing my helpless state.

Many books I read, many paths I trod,
Now save the Lord, they're not worth the nod.

Smitten to affiance with ways of a froward,
I know I was but a babbling coward,

Untouched by shame for sins committed,
Decoyed by vain whims so easily permitted.


Un-repenting for actions indiscreet,
I blasphemed the bless-ed Paraclete.


Too callous to be hurt by bible scorn,
I hid in the guise of self adorn.


Unable to refrain from wicked speech,
I welcomed gossip's daring breach.


Thinking to be stable, unchanging intents,
I was as a corpse that naturally ferments.


Often-times in solitude I yearn to create,
Forgive me Lord, your grace I belate.


Eating and sleeping poetic entice,
Dear Lord, expel this joyous vice


So your love made external remains internal,
Gaining protection from the devil's inferno.


Often-times elated by earth's scenic beauty,
I again neglected a mighty gratuity,


For joys are fleeting from things created,
Ill-pleasing the Father, the Un-Created!

Many times I thought to believe in the Lord,
Except when I met the villian's sword.

Basking in the sunshine over a godsent past,
I cleaved unto the Lord for pearls He cast;

Yet melted into reverie for breach of trust
When my fortune was not so fair and just.

Oh Divinity, once again you answer my call,
And caress a memory of pleasant recall,

For thinking love I'm no longer apart,
No sooner I'm fanned by a subtle heart.

In her eyes formed a radiant gleam
That seemed eminent from early pristine.

Feeling an affinity, I knew she caressed
My timidity, as blushes clearly confessed.

Thinking nature's best and I no longer
In tune, I pampered her, fearing to wrong her.

Bereft of hope no longer was I;
Again I confided in heaven's high.

Imaging her atop a gallant mountain side,
All thoughts of love reached their tide:

"So many hours apart we spent, I sensed
No better beauty the cosmic could dare dispense.

Often thinking the cosmos and I were scorned,
Nothing more nourishing could I adorn.

Like chirping (s) of cocks send visions saintly,
Tickering of her heart softly acquaints - me

With sounds of sweet, borning lull's of incense,
While arousing a closeness that bids scorn for pretense.

Alone we were, flattering not,
For how, when such blooming springs un-knot.

The mood of fine hour's twilight sends our
Imaginations soaring on tower.

Erupting with brilliancy was not only a star,
But all nature glistens as our fancies ajar."

Long-lasting silence finally broken,
And I, relishing the flowering token,

Scanned the bosom of the moon-lit universe,
And uttered secretly a heart-felt verse:

"Wondrous I received your fair eyes gleam
With all that sparkles can esteem.

So cared the cast of your wind-blown hair,
But more is its effulgent glare.

Passage-way, so hidden and rare to see,
Plainly known cuz you glow in modesty.

Splendor I see in your tender legs bare
As they clear openings in the air,

Then entranced I become when felt are caresses
Of your fair-legs flesh; still not my finesse.

Most enravishing though is your angelic appearance,
Never lacking impact even after your disappearance."

So reads the verse, and afterwards tears flowed
Down her cheeks making a small-sized row

With all that joy could lavishly give
Wanting an eternity in the present to live.

Upon calming, she whispered, "Our verse to cherish,
Debarred from stains that beg it perish,

Just as blossoms in you and I
Bud forth, praying for life on High,

As we feed off the blitzing sun,
Becoming enraptured, then eternally one."

Betrayed I sensed not, because now I'm apart
Of a blossomed lot that's flattered from start.

Toil now settling to a mere whimper,
Off we went into the white-laden winter,

Where regions briskly hushed and scant,
Offered a quiet much suiting embracement.

Recomforted by my heavenly encounter, I beseemed
An urge to wander from my long yearned dream,

And pondered and pondered my baffling affair,
Wishing release from joys unfair.

Satiety lurking my amorous intrigue,
Heralded love's most sombre critique.

Again disenchantment I find, could it be
I was victim of deception's frolic spree?

"Indubitably so," uttered my awakening
Inner voice, "For you being so taken

With mundane desire, fled beauteous attire,
And thinking to grasp your earthly squire,

Ensnared cunning with all that joy could give,
And fathomed asunder with but a yearn to live."

True, but why does it appear at first
Like an embellishing bloom un-curst?

Because it's nature's flaming intoxicant to prevent
Everlasting gloom's hapless torment!

More and more tiring of earthly dark,
Fleeting joy and hypnotic stark,

I fervently retired into a sepulchral muse,
And seeking to stamp out further abuse,

Renounced my illusive lady, yearning now,
Celestial portal's vibrant prow.

Chaste I became, psychic energy I stored,
Knowledge on High lured and soared,

And hell-bred trivia, now held at bay,
Harbored an energy that could still any day.

More soothed I became attempting to breed
A smothered and starved celestial seed,

But sweltering torpidities of besetting events
Leaped from suspension ushering new intents.

Thus now see much joy in distress,
For of the Lord, I think and address.

## A Child is born

Starving by wants of joys to share,
I wilted underneath my fruitless care;

Lest I would have cried out loud,
Boasting of the Lord His bursting shroud.

Under the guise of all I suffer,
Are blessings from God, the soothing buffer.

Religion, monasteries, Saint Benedict's rule,
Not for me, it seemed so cruel;

Though hours I wept when learning my betroth
To the heathen's way was a favor to sloth.

Converts of past seemed unworthy to revere,
But now I pray they persevere.

Confessions I made, I hope not to the devil,
Else I'll be doomed on a hellish level.

I present these confessions to the world
So I can share a joy now hurled

Through Jesus Christ, my consoling elixir,
And quintessent companion in battling the
                                        vexer.

Wilt Thou forgive a long lost soul
That's wearied without Thy fair Condole?

Whatever the answer, I eagerly await,
Praying deliverance from Trials of Fate!

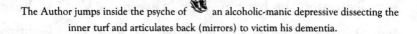

The Author jumps inside the psyche of an alcoholic-manic depressive dissecting the inner turf and articulates back (mirrors) to victim his dementia.

## Dear Darryl,

I am the juggler man from alcatraz. Give me a Vod in one hand and a bible in the other and watch me teeter and teeter, finally totter, usually the Vod wins out; I laugh, "see Bible you ain't got that hold on me any more;" I mock you but I got my Vod; I suck and suck; no more teat to suckle; AH, I now got my Vod; it sends me so far adrift all gone the worries; I got my Vod! Such a loveless wretch I am I even hate myself more than others; Beyond my own height I can never see; If I see hate in me I cannot help but direct hate to another; Yes, Beyond my own height I cannot see. My poor sister Sarah, she the toilet, I am the Stool; The stench is rancid I pass onto her; Oh but she's strong I quip to myself, she can take it but does she know I never mean the things I say to her; I feel so guilt ridden, sleepless nights ravage my days over why I persist in lashing out toward her. I asked Ronne if the cause could be that now that John is dead could I be taking it out on him. I wish I was dead, my frequent ponder. My soul is the devil's plaything. My heart goes out to Mom, the hell with everyone else; screw'm; I applaud my lingo, after all, Zane Gray is my mentor; John Wayne is my idol and Wyatt Earp is my Burp. Give me a 45 and a western town and I'll blow up every structure, every person in sight Rambo style cuz you see, I am a wretched man; I thrive on destruction, the devils glory; I pull up my stool drop my elbow atop the bar top, blurt "Give me a Vod" so I can poison my senses over this latest bar room hurrah. Guilt so ravages my heart over my sickness, my sickly acts; my pitiless attacks upon my sister, Sarah. Ronne says it's a good sign; at least I have the seed; the seed of conscience. The Work teachings will assist my development of REAL conscience Ronne says to me. I hope it will cuz these teachings are a rare find, a profound necessity for a wretched fool, as I am the Juggler man from Alcatraz.

Damn my wretched yearn for Vod, Sir Vod, that is, when will it ever end; is death my only salvage? Ronne says premature death will be a certain guarantee that I will continue drinking even after expiration as I will voraciously seek out other living physical bodies who have my weakness for alcohol and I will possess them to satisfy my craving with one catch; indeed, one very major catch; I will not be able to satisfy my craving/thirst and since their is no physical body I could not even hope for death to destroy the urge. And now comes the spiritual law; I will drink drink drink drink drink drink for the period of time I was destined to live on earth naturally without experiencing craving gratification. Such a hellish thought. That Ronne sure makes me think. I am so stupid; I am a dullard; My brain is a gelatinous mass of matter spiked with ethanol and whatever

toxic substance you can think; Afterall, for so many years I ate
like a Hog. I wish Sarah and I could talk together, instead of
AT each other. I know she has done well by me over the
frolicsome years I have put her through and April through and
yet I treat them both with disdain. Why is that Ronne? Why
is that Ronne? Why is that Ronne? Such a wretched damning
creature I am, especially, in lieu of the book knowledge I have
been exposed to. I know I have not internalized ANY of it; but
maybe some day the miracle will occur for my two sisters to see.
That will be nectar to my soul and freedom to my heart. My
heart is now cracked and only a cracked heart boasts an
opening for entry of the Divine. Please God, don't let the devil
manipulate me like I manipulate others. I treat Sarah like a dog
and my bark oftentimes draws blood. In truth, I am the dog
and she is the leader. I gave up my inherent reign for
intoxication. So successful, both my sisters are; I am the blind
dog living in a maze (some would say daze) without them by my
side I would have off'd my life long ago, I ponder. I am the
little slave; they are my surrogates; I feel so puny before them;
my ego so shattered; Oh lord, where can I muster the courage
to say I am sorry for all my misdeeds that I appreciate you
being there for me. How can I be worthy being in the company
of April amid such intense emasculation. I am not a man; I am
more of a child than my own girl. Does anyone understand???
At least why could not my sisters be older than I? Then I would
not have to shoulder the image "I am the older brother imbibed
to look after them. "Damn my wretched yearn for Sir Vod

Himself!! Juggle Juggle Juggle the Juggernaut. I mean no harm to others; How do I front affectations, dear Lord; show me the way else I will end up in a dumpster packed away for sewage broth. Ronne tells me to pay attention to women they are better at it than men. Why am I so frightened of my own feminine side? A private question only I know of. I read it takes courage to be soft and discernment to know when to be tough. Why do I have to be tough (ACT) tough without discrimination all to often i.e before my friends, associates and last, but not least, my sisters? I am not like them unconscionable fools that sleep beside me in my jail cell; then what am I doing in there when I know better. Am I so weakened from years of interior abuse that I cannot see the forest from the trees. Indeed, I am a ostrich with his head buried in the sand. Ronne knows me; Sarah knows me; they can penetrate the sand granules that have sanded my grey matter down to nothing but one mass of sandstone; gelatinous inebriate that I am. Hide and seek I called it as a youngster. Now as an adult I strut the earth in various lost and found departments being pandied about as a common dog. Oh Lord, Is Gurdjieff right, does undeveloped man die like a DOG!!! Please, Lord, give me the strength to lift my head out of the sand and sink it into the WORK teachings. I am not a dog; I beseech, I am more than a dog; I am surrounded by blessedness something my cell mates cannot boast. I have financial well being; I have Sarah to handle my petty responsibilities; I have friends to talk to; I have a humble abode; I have it all except

Love; I am a loveless wretch. How could I boast a love for others when not hate, but indifference, is the menu I cook up for myself. I read over and over that love is tantamount to enlightenment i. e the spirit of charity. What charity do I harbor when I send out a thank you note to one of the nurses from the jail when my sister is the brunt of my recent brutishness, ideally worthy of said note, as I have admitted to Ronne, but My bones are not humble, says Ronne. Expressions of tenderness are so hard for me to corral; Am I justified in blaming John for that? I hear I must forget the past that's true forgiveness! Do I have the strength to be weak. I must resolve this anomaly now. I am so kind to strangers but to those whom I owe psychological debts to I am so brutish. Could it be I harbor the thought that the world is my OYSTER AND THAT I HAVE NO DEBT TO SOCIETY; TO GOD, TO PAY BACK!?! I will talk to Ronne about that one. It's a frightening realization to ponder the thought that I am a mere earthen parasite.

JUGGLE     JUGGLE     JUGGLE
THE   JUGGERNAUT


FLIP ME A VOD,
NOPE, FLIP ME A PAGE;
NOPE, I'M A MERE CLOD
NOT A SAGE!!!

FLIP ME A VOD;
NOPE, I MUST CALL SARAH
I'M NOT A CLOD,
I NEED APRIL TOO!

FLIP ME A VOD,
NOPE, I WANT MY SON;
I PRAY HE GIVES THE NOD;
SO TOGETHER WE FUN AND FUN!

FLIP ME A VOD;
NOPE, A LIVING GHOST FOLLOWS ME ABOUT;
HE'S MY DAD, I GIVE THE NOD,
FROM THE ROOF I NOW CAN SHOUT!!!

FLIP ME A VOD;
NOPE, I MUST SILENCE MY SHOUT;
ELSE MY FAMILY SQUAD
WILL THINK I LOST MY MACHO CLOUT!

FLIP ME A VOD;
FLIP ME A VOD;
OH GOD, OH GOD,
DON'T LET ME NOD!!!

I am the Schizoid Man
Par excellence;
My secret longing in life
Is to witness a shoot out
    At the O K Corral
        BETWEEN
    GOD and SATAN! ! !

Laughter Laughter Laughter
I am a cowboy at heart;
Where did my financial acumen
Come from anyway?
Cowboys live from ranch to ranch
Food morsel to food morsel;
Camp fire to camp fire,
Thoughtless of the day to follow.

I am the preacher man,
The western plains I scout;
I wear the cape
And all the Garb;
I scout and scout and scout
Looking for cowhands to preach to.

My sermons cover one subject;
LIFE IS A COSMIC JOKE! ! !

A wise guy in the audience notices;
My mind is teetering to and fro
I trip over the air
That got in the way;
Where's my VOD
I whisper to myself?
I ponder; Sarah took it;
No Ronne took it;
No April took it this time.
I feel so naked without my stilt.
ANY-WAY, THE WISE GUY SAYS TO ME;
If life is a cosmic joke
Then why do you take it so serious
Preacher Man par excellence?
Stunned and choked I gazed emptily;
The wise guy embellishes his words;
You, preacher man, are the one that takes life so serious
Else why must you dull your senses
With Satan's nectar
When God's nectar is free
Just for the asking
And fosters peace
Not inner torment!
YOU ARE A HYPOCRITE, PREACHER MAN!
GET ON YOUR HORSE
GET OUT OF OUR TOWN;
FEAR NOT, HE ADDS,

YOUR HORSE IS SOBER;
A STRAIGHT LINE HE CAN TROD!


I long for a new jail cell to settle in;
There, I am the king.
After all, palsied fools are my company;
I gloat, my gelatinous brain
Is still sharper than their's.


YOU SEE, I AM THE JOHN WAYNE OF THE WEST;
I AM THE BILLY GRAHAM OF THE WEST;
I AM THE BHAGWAN RAGNEESH OF THE EARTH!


                    YOU SEE


I AM BILLY THE KID INCARNATE ! ! !
DOUBT ME BUSTER,
I BLOW THAT GUN RIGHT OUT YOUR HOLSTER
AND POUNCE MY STIRRUP ON YOUR ADAM'S
                                        APPLE;
YOUR BLOOD IS MY GUTS! ! !

I am not a bad man. Why cannot I grapple my pangs of destructiveness? Please, Lord, send down one of your angels with a post hole digger to ream my arteries of ethanol and while you're at it bring down some grey matter to reconvolute my brain. I heard brain transplant is not possible so at least give me some gray matter to provide me a new substance; convolutions, else I boast a mere elephant brain; no convolutions to absorb an iota of truth serum I am continually exposed to viz a viz Work teaching books. I heard from Lucifer during the dark of night that this is my only hope for sanity restoration. I want so much to be grounded; my daze is not a phase, it appears it will last forever anon; can you help me? I am a helpless rapidly degenerating man? Ronne tells me these very thoughts presage a hope as a glimmering flicker of Essence is shining forth throughout my being that the Prince of darkness has not yet suffocated me; Dowsed my inner light. Elsewise my hapless condition would make Satan MOURN!

My sisters bring out the devil in me; why is that Ronne? He says cuz they, like your father, know you so well; all your tricks; they have, in short, entered you psychically; psychic surgeons call them, blameless they are, indeed, for they love their sickly brother unconditionally, just as Mom did SO MUCH! Ronne further says a danger zone is always entered when interior guts are exposed to another for the stench would make a skunk choke. Emptiness, Emptiness, Emptiness, Emptiness, Emptiness, Emptiness, Emptiness, is a reality. Ronne says that we must all come to grip with this fact so that when all of our DEPENDENT ARISINGS MANIFEST THEMSELVES then disappear (loss of loved ones for ex.) we will not feel the loss of a psychological appendage. In truth, Essence is only Real, Emptiness is the Chairman of the Board and fullness is the Flowery messenger. A great hazard for those who aspire a expanded inner life is that parody will always reign; Realness is always a contradiction hence the fine line between genius and insanity. Kill me! Kill me somebody! my emptiness is frightening me to death impulse when the opposite should occur. Gripping my emptiness should render me buoyant with life; as light as a bubbly, dancing, whirling child.

I cannot accept the shear futility of life. I am a fraud. My personality is a fake, a false mask that survived the harangue of all my early life conditioning by well meaning, but ignorant impostors. The blind made me even more blind than they; I, therefore, have chosen my Path to enlightenment; The epitaph reads aloud; the vibrations boast a common theme song; MY PATH IS THE PATH OF B L A M E! ! ! ! ! ! THANK GOD THOSE WHO JUSTIFY DO NOT CONVINCE else everyone would think as I do and the entire world would be destroyed, one prodigious soup bowl filled with blood and guts.

I want so much to land aground safely; can my family land me safely; can they forgive me my mental derangement. Where is MOM when I need her; She is safe in Heaven I portend;

Dad is a living Ghost he harmed me greatly I IMAGINED. Can a truce ever be felt? Can a truce ever be felt? Can a truce ever be felt? Is John really my Dad? After all he sported the white drop that met Mom's red drop to make me. Ronne tells me I chose my parents as the spirit forever guides one's selection process on the inner planes after death and before birth and the choice is predicated upon the most ideally suited situation, i.e. parents to advance one's spiritual evolution. I SHOULD BE THANKFUL, RONNE TELLS, ME, FOR EVERYTHING EVEN MY SUFFERING FOR IT'S A HEAVENLY PRIVILEGE TO BE ABLE TO WORK OFF ONE'S KARMIC DEBTS/OBLIGATIONS WHILE STILL IN THE PHYSICAL BODY! Please Lord, [i] beseech [YOU] to exorcise the dragon that whittles and whittles and whittles away at my individual Will. I have no will left the miserable creature has bitten it to death. I am a mere automaton flitting and wavering bottomsy turvy in the wind. Flick me with your finger I will topple. I can't tell my brawling bar buddies that: they think I'm king of the street with a license to destroy viz a viz my certified insanity. Ragneesh is my certifier, after all, he proclaimed his own madness.

In my rocky heart I know there is hope for me; so many others have been worse off than me and look at them decades later leading productive maybe even spiritually assertive lives. PLEASE LIGHT MY FIRE SOMEBODY I'm not ashes yet. Forgive me my sins and TRESPASSES EVERYBODY; Oh

Lord please listen. I am culpable but not intentional. I envy those who have not my addictions; who have not my coldness of heart; who have a Dad; Where hath the white drop gone? So far away it seems. Please let me find it somebody, anybody who will listen.

I now end this epitaph abruptly. I pray that my life on earth is not ended so abruptly. Please Lord  never forsake me. I read Your script always trying and trying to decipher; to break your Code!

I AM  THE  J U G G L E R  M A N ! ! !
F R O M  A L C A T R A ! ! !Z

[ And I am the Juggleteur]

Sincerely Mine,

# A Letter To a Young Woman

## A brief introduction to Gurdjieff - Ouspensky Teachings

Psycho - Spiritual commentaries on the inner life with a brief introduction to Gurdjieff - Ouspensky Teachings.

Dear Katerina;

And now we come to the next task for this day; for this moment; the only moment that will ever be; ever is. Let's see where this note leads to: A dawning of sped up thought streams scanned my being when I observed your mother\father espouse a waking dream symbol for me to heed. Her gift of book ends, cemented my tentative pondering(s) regarding what could I do for Katerina , who brought home to pasture, within me solace and gaiety. For that, thoughts of gratitude filled my cup of good fortune. I looked across my room being eyed by stacks of books selectively purchased especially for you; a symbol and tribute you may well transcend as your career election of mental medicine or psychology is nearing its launching pad. Solace churned my being when it was learned that you were entering the field of psychology as opposed to the originally intended business administration field for reasons I already expressed !

As you browse the book titles a charming title you will not find. These books are real work on self books; the corollary being the wellness of others; for the benefit of Beings everywhere even lessening the suffering of God (Brief notes attached to books suggest a reading sequence to extract better comprehension. This applies to Work books.) I've been studying books on psychology, philosophy and the like since the age of thirteen always curious about mental abstractions and the barbaric nature of the adult world. I was fortunate to have stumbled upon the Work teachings (Gurdjieff- Ouspensky and their students) at the early age of twenty-one. The average age of students is forty-ish. An entire new vocabulary will be required to unravel the meaning of the teachings a true rendition of Esoteric Christianity. (Not all books are on the Work.)

Jesus was a master therapist/teacher His primal forum: Man must awaken from sleep! He spoke this aloud continually to others. Parables, parables and more parables were His forte, indeed, feigning His true intent, namely, to coerce one into the waking state via the creation of a shroud of mystery to separate the sincere seekers from the casual curiosity mongers. He knew, as you will learn from study, that this work is not for the light of heart. A complete aborting of psychological BUFFERS must be borne. The waking state is a rare state (it need not be) and when it is experienced one knows unequivocally they have entered into a higher dimension of perception. Once the ideas are grasped/internalized years and years of continual incidents of self remembering (Books elaborate-Katerina) are needed to DE-AUTOMATIZE the human biological machine.

Dissecting, assimilating and practicing the Work teachings will imbibe in Katerina the likely position of a therapist's therapist. Not being privy to speak with you on a level other than politeness it is a bit difficult to assess the nature of the proliferating questions you must harbor. Anyone bespeaking an interest in the inner sciences is truly a walking question mark; indeed, a tribute to your introspective nature-your physiognomy reveals the kinship. The seeming insurmountable task in grasping the Work is the primary unbending thought in seekers is that one is already AWAKE, else how could one carry on with the individual tasks of day to day living! In short Katerina, I'm confident in asserting you will espouse an early grip on the countless venerable and not so venerable exigencies of life's chess game arming your being with inner and intrapersonal advantages if you study the Work. Caution: An early grasping of the Work ideas will likely cause complications in relationships with men as perforce your inner perceptions escalate (once initial shock is experienced transporting you to another octave) (can't describe with words) and rare is the man who will submit to a rapidly evolving soul. This latter comment is necessary and responsible.

Gurdjieff always demanded that his students be single or, if married, attend the school with the mate. Once the initial shock strikes one's being, a life as it WAS, is no more. That law, in no uncertain terms, is immutable. Contrariwise, if one mate catches the disease ( the dis-Ease) of knowing, in heart, the difference between the waking state and the sleep state and the other merely looks on, jealousy lurks, to name but a few of the negative emotions that will manifest.

The Work does not waste time on rubble of past that's for the menu of the psychology field to explore/often times even exploit. Study Body-Centered psychotherapy for the virtue of momentariness in therapy sessions. (A Book enclosed, Katerina.) Consider an analogy to further explain uselessness of dissecting past experiences: Imagine a cup of water filled to brim with salt granules. They lie dormant at bottom of glass. Shake up the glass, all granules then float about within the confines of the glass (no one can rise above their own height-granules will not rise above the glass proper as their is no medium (body) for doing so. Hence the futility in trying to bring up the sludge through mental coercion, or manipulation. No mortal can perform that task on another for the law of karma (you reap what you sow) is firmly embedded where it belongs down deep (bottom of glass) so one can fill the circles marked by heaven. A premature shaking does naught but muddy the container-glass. So often, under the guise of professionalism the content is mistaken for the container. You must of heard of the statement "Can't see the forest from the Trees." The latter two maxims are similar in meaning. There is a special meditation called Dynamics, a profoundly active meditative device to forge a purging of past rubble created by Osho Rajneesh years ago that is slowly making its way into the ranks of therapists around the world as, indeed effective. (I enclosed several books by him.) Jesus taught the Light and Sound method to forge a purging, i.e the entry of the Holy spirit rears its comforting tentacles in the GUISE of viewing a VISIBLE LIGHT AND AUDIBLE SOUND/MELODY VIA THE BLESSING OF THE "SINGLE EYE" "TENTH DOOR"! The eye and door are the words of Jesus that priests have zero knowledge of. The eastern religions call it the Third eye; Tisra Til; all the ancient holy scripts have there own terminology vouchsafing criticalness of softening/opening these doors for the holy spirit to perform its work, its Comforting-says Jesus erewhile purifying/perfecting us to render one worthy of transport to the heaven worlds even while still in the BODY! PAUL the apostle: "Out of body or no." So many wondrous truths are WOVEN within the pages of holy writings. Indeed, Katerina, there is a wondrous KINGDOM OF HEAVEN within us; within our Temple "Made without sound of Hammer" Go to church made without sound of hammer says, Jesus. Yet imagine the compendium of idiocy lurking through temples made with sound of Hammer. Consider many thousand of cases of child molestation/homosexuality amongst priests all because of a lack of knowledge on HOW TO SUBLIMATE SEX ENERGY. Indeed, the Human biological machine is our true and blessed transformational apparatus; our vehicle to exit; to vacate the prison of the body; i.e being possessed by the play of flesh passions. I'm off on some kind of tangent, Katerina, but then I'm writing in stream of consciousness fashion so no holds barred, I self elect.

I sense a need for a retrace regarding the manipulation and coercion by others to unravel the past idiom. The entire contingent is predicated upon the narcissistic preoccupation to BLAME OTHERS!! The Work explicity teaches, (unless one transcends the penchant for internal considering ( a Work term) or constant tally of a personal accounting system) the transcending of negative emotions is impossible. The life of BLAME and ever riotous compulsion for INTER- personal accounting (you did that to me; I'm gonna get back at ya recording plants its indelible imprint on the akashic record ( a cosmic memory of each and every detail of one's life.) Jesus says even each of individual hairs are numbered. The exorcism of residue from this driven pass time of white sheep begins in gradated increments as one does practical work on oneself. The swamp land of Mind, a useful tool for the non-sleeping human biological machine, but with a natural propensity to avoid resistance (bouts of de-automation or discipline) mind becomes a vicious compendium of unuseable food; It cowers to one's "Sacred Impulse" to Voluntarize their Human Biological Machine, the Temple of God!! With each downed attempt to de-automate, chances in one particular lifetime, grow ever more remote. The primal HAZARD: *A person can work on themselves* (change-advance-evolve) *when in the waking state only.* Imagine: It is not the *Essence/*person that is asleep, instead, it is the Human biological machine that is asleep.

(This is a pearl Katerina and deserves unrelenting desire to comprehend.) It is one's I D E N T I F I C A T I O N with the sleeping machine that paves one's road to Hell! Never will Katerina find a more concise extrapolation of the phenomena of IDENTIFICATION than in her WORK Study!!! It's a profoundly insidious occurrence catching one completely unawares...!! An example to ponder; Become like little children, Jesus admonished. Well, here is why: A two year old (Still in the first octave of Life) is told he/she must wait until next week to acquire a certain gift. A week hence seems light years to a child. Their sense of moment to moment preoccupation is profound and a delight to watch. One Christmas to the next seems a multiplied millennium to one so young and vibrating; so buoyant; indeed, the seven seals (chakras-transparent wheels of energy located along the) STRAIT-spine spin at a pace propelled by the Might of God! (see the Hands of light Book enclosed, Katerina.) Contrariwise, as adults progress in years, the enclosure from one year end to another grows ever smaller. The illusion of time speeds up, so it seems! It is, in fact, our identification with the body and all of its ancillary habits that accelerate creating the illusion of a contracted SPACE TIME CONTINUUM; i.e it seems like yesterday I was 20 yrs old. An even better model exemplifying one's identification with body goes as follows: Katerina has her first client/patient; she espouses her inner pain mentioning various persons responsible; (the usual epitaph, anyway) She cites an incident trod by an employer, he lashing out callous condemnations toward her. Her pain is proliferating. Katerina interjects, ( her name will be Laurie) now Laurie, listen carefully to what I'm about to suggest to you; "YOUR BOSS ATTACKED LAURIE NOT YOU!! YOU ARE NOT LAURIE; YOU ARE NOT LAURIE ; YOU ARE Y O U!! A PERFECTLY IMPERFECT CHILD OF GOD! SOUL IS IMPERVIOUS TO EFFECTS OF OUTER WORLD; YOU ARE SOUL; Y O U A R E    Y O U ! !   YOU ARE NOT LAURIE; THAT PERSON LAURIE IS    A  MIND  CREATION;  AN ILLUSION; THE AGGRESSOR IS MERELY ASLEEP; HE LIKEWISE IS NOT HIS NAME; HE IS SOUL; NOT EVEN A SOUL; BUT SOUL PERSONIFIED ! ! The term a soul presumes we are separate; WE ARE ONE! Katerina. I present this example not to oversimplify individual problems, but they are truly self created via the process of identification. Above is not necessarily a suggested therapeutic approach in an institutional setting as it will come across as being callous, un-nurturing and besides, for sleeping humanity, coddling is required to keep in tack their psychological buffers. The Work is not for the light of heart. It is not for those content to live their days eating, sleeping, and screwing; The trinity of life is for the walking DEAD!

Their is an enemy to the waking state. That enemy is the Chronic. As soon as the temple is on the verge of awakening the chronic is activated to keep the snooze of the temple

(Human biological machine as a transformational apparatus) dominant making the struggle all the greater to awaken; to deautomate one's response to external stimuli! This struggle is the welfare of those seekers in the Work for they thrive on the friction of life's play (Maya) for it is only then that one can acquire/accumulate food stuff to nourish SOUL! *To sculpt soul! The crap of life is clay for the soul sculptor!!!* Most wish to eat nourishing food to make waste; True seekers oblige the crap of life to T R A N S F O R M it into useable data/soul substances to develop body kesdjan (higher bodies) our inherited vehicles of transport to the invisible worlds. Invisible to the two external eyes but not the inner eye! The single eye; or third eye as taught in all of the ancient holy scriptures. Freud would call the chronic a defense mechanism. Freud was not conscious of Work teaching. In fact , he never even discovered the sub-un-conscious; it was his mentor Fyodor Dostoyevsky who did! Freud studied his novels. Dostoyevsky's "Notes from the Underground" short story is a profound study of man. You may wish to read it. I recall reading hundreds of novels by the masters of literature in my younger years. Unforgettable reads and an ideal foundation for the inner journey.

I intuit you, Katerina, sense their is something seriously wrong with so called humans (I don't mean crime and all that stuff, that's mere Karma flaming and burn off.) I mean the overt nature of beings in general. Is it truly adequate that we live and die like dogs? (Jesus refers to sleeping humans as goats). Does Katerina ever ponder how beings are so accepting being imprisoned by their bodies and concomitant passions? It is our obligation to God to rise above body consciousness, however charming, the snares may be. The body/Temple is the greatest gift from God/Absolute we could have and to imagine it is *our* body is a shameless psychological misnomer. The body is a present "a gift from on high," to abuse it is a travesty fostering grave consequences; it can be taken from us at any time; for even that time is numbered (Jesus) hence the terror of the situation ( a work term.) If my father gave me a gift, even a crumb size in comparison, I could not rear it back in his face. That is what we do to Our Father which art in heaven when temple/body abuse ensues. The men of the cloth are not to keen on the apostle's words (Faith without works is undone) for it takes away from the virtue of psycho prayer babble mechanically expressed by sleepers-somnambulists. Prayer inside the Waking state is ecstatic; otherwise, it's shameless vanity. So much money is made off the Dead! Where have the teachings of Jesus and other masters disappeared to, anyway? Knowing we have the potential to rise above the body through a voluntary creation of alignment with higher, invisible, forces should solace any soul. These forces, upon proper alignment, will, indeed, catapult one's soul into other worlds (to vast a subject to elaborate on in this note). Actually, as one looks down from above (silver cord attached to prevent actual death) saying to him/herself, "You mean that is me down there, that blob of flesh; Oh it's so wonderful up here (out of

Body) do I have to return, is the beginning response." Paul the Apostle; "Out of Body or No." Nothing new, is or will ever be, said under the sun, even Jesus said that, Katerina. The secret road maps are coyly hidden within the ancient holy texts for pearls canst not be cast before Swine, says Jesus. The experience of being out of body is a wondrous journey into the far country, surely, a life changing event in the seeker. As soul undergoes the voluntary sculpting process, fired by the intentional yearn to perfect Itself, (outer world perfectionists live in hell on earth and occupy in mass the mental hospitals-they will be your clients/patients for the most part) the heavenly kingdom within delivers its nectar; indeed, heaven on earth; in the world but not of it viz a viz one's impassioned urge to intentionally suffer (Take up the cross) not the ever so common un-intentional suffering common amongst sheep; Self remembering is a form of intentional suffering. Self remembering is a term that may appear self explanatory. Assuredly, that is not the case. In fact, it takes considerable work on oneself to transport one's consciousness into a self remembered MODE during an emotional attack by another. Self remembering is double arrowed attention (you observe yourself observing another, simultaneously, observing the other observing; (the observer become the observed and vice versa plus simultaneously cognizant of the Absolute (God) looking down upon you; ideally *thrice arrowed attention!* Jesus references the term Witness i.e imagine the cursor planted on the screen of your consciousness skating upward looking down upon you (That's witnessing your actions) (work books and Osho books) expound on the phenomena and its criticalness to expanding consciousness. It's impossible to express negative emotions when in this state of self remembering, Katerina! There are little exercises that one can do through the day to exercise the attention muscles in small increments i.e starting with observing the movements of the body (moving brain-work term) since if one cannot self remember while attending to the movements of the body which moves at a relatively slow pace, then the faster paced intellectual brain (work term) will send one into a myriad of likes and dislikes (a trait of the intellectual brain) i.e one feels as though they are running around like a chicken with its head off. The emotional brain (work term) moves at a pace far in excess as the subtlety of moods/emotions creep up on one unawares. Consider, thought travels at approximately one million miles per second i.e the habit experienced in the intellectual brain and the reality of such speed can be felt first hand once one has experienced SOUL exiting-vacating the body (out of Body) since the space time continuum is voided. Once one's in the void; the abyss of emptiness, the mush of the body accumulations is gone. Now consider the super express prevalent in the emotional brain(located at the right side of heart,) "Multiply a thousand fold its speed of emotions relative to the speed of thought and you can easily understand why emotions possess; dominate and destroy sleeping humanity. The ideal of the work teachings is to be in all three brains simultaneously; this is a expanded form of self remembering!!!  I choose to merely touch the surface, Katerina, the enclosed books will assist you in comprehending the virtues of self remembering.

Instead of self remembering, the disease of tomorrow SELF CALMS the being, further channeling sloth.  Buffered by the charms of Mortal life's day to day screen plays (the nectar of death) one succumbs to the ever prevalent illusion of Tomorrowness called Retirement! By that time, the human biological machine is so automated and creaky the pearl beyond PRICE becomes so buried beneath the rubble of a dualistic life (for every pleasure there will be an equal pain-if not immediate then later) the balls and chains are firmly in place.  This dichotomous anomaly and merciless pattern of Sir nature only applies to mortal life on earth, Whereas in the heaven world, duality is dissolved by the energy of third force, the <u>neutralizer.</u> Third force is a Work term and deserves much study.  The line of least resistance is the password for merrymakers; the line of most resistance is the script of sincere seekers as they know, intuitively, their inner voice echoes:" My child, wait, the grass will eventually grow by itself."And what appeared to be resistance, initially, is dissolved by POTENCY OF THRICE ARROWED ATTENTION!!! Consequently, the secret parody of it all is that those who CHOSE THEIR SUFFERING don't suffer at all. "My burden is light; my yoke is easy" says Jesus! The longer the human biological machine lays in wait for that magic day, lukewarmness, grows more calming to  the machine squelching to death any hope for salvation (in this lifetime anyway) from the ravages of an out of control biological machine! As karmic rectitude ("reap what you sow"- Jesus) clasps its ugly hand another lifetime, another go around on the wheel of Dharma is required to get the HINT! The wheel of Dharma keeps -a-spinning and is Sir Nature happy, for the successful, freely spinning of its HUB is contingent upon the sleeping human biological machine, the PERFECT servant of Sir Nature!!! Its bearings, being so heavily oiled by the play of negative emotions, one's only hope is the invading "COMFORTER"- Jesus emitting its tentacles in the form OF THE VISIBLE LIGHT AND AUDIBLE SOUND CURRENT!!! This trinity, Katerina, is the HOLY SPIRIT emanating its ambrosia; The sound current being the Chairman of the board; The light, being the President and the Comforter being the SECRETARY!!!

Yes, there ARE certain ways to open/soften the Single eye located between the two outer eyes a slight above the brow line-PINEAL Gland and sensitize the inner ear! Not within the scope of this note to expound, however.

Before closing out this note I have to make one more retrace. Recall the hypothetical therapy sessions expounding the relevance of the idea ONE IS NOT THEIR BODY. If Katerina should have a rape victim, said rape victim, because of penetration of her physical body, by rapist even, her ASTRAL

ENVELOPE-BODY SHE WOULD BE TAKING ON SOME OF THE KARMA OF HER AGGRESSOR AND THAT IS PROFOUNDLY HAZARDOUS TO HER EVOLUTION AS SOUL! HER LIKELY IGNORANCE OF THIS SPIRITUAL LAW is a Blessing. A literal puncturing of astral bodies occur between lovers which is why the sensation is so relieving, but the consequences are so enormous. The consequence of aids is pale in comparison. [A woman is like a sponge to the energy of her mate;] metaphysically magnetic and biologically receptive, consequently, the hazard of INTERchange of karmic interface is considerably greater for her. Jesus calls the sexual fluids THE GOLDEN OIL; IT IS THIS OIL THAT IS NEEDED TO RISE UP THE STRAIT. Notice scriptural spelling of strait which means like a strait over water OR SPINE OILING THE SINGLE EYE; THE THIRD EYE ; THE TENTH DOOR!!! The loss of one drop of seminal fluid is equivalent to losing one pint of BLOOD!THE UNCANNY FORCE OF ATTENTION IS THE MOTOR TO PROPEL IN MOTION THE ORBIT OF SEX ENERGY FROM THE LOWER PERINEUM up to Pituitary and back down. This is one microcosmic orbit that spins faster than light. When this energy is "dormant," i.e lying down at the perineum (muladhara chakra-situated between the anus and scrotum or vaginal opening) sex urges ravage the sleeping biological machine. [So actually, sex urges are a result of deadened sex force contrary to what is commonly thought by majority.] The purposeful circulation of this sex energy is one secret to rising above body domination. Katerina, this is a complicated subject and I think I had better stop here. So many variances enter into proper instruction in this esoteric matter. I mentioned it because in your profession sexuality will be upper most importance in therapy. The western culture knows very little about sexuality!!! I did not enclose the follow book (Cultivating female sexuality-Mantak Chia) because I felt you could purchase that one on your own. You will acquire advanced knowledge by reading it. There is potential hazard in activating lower chakras, Katerina! If you tinker you will need guidance.

Katerina, if I thought you to be a promiscuous woman I would have not have, number one: even typed this note; nor would I have exposed you to latter knowledge pertaining to sex energy. "Let the Dead bury the dead. " The law of Non-Interference is important and practical. As far as I know you may already have some knowledge of these matters.

Recall I referenced the emotional brain. Within this emotional brain is a lower and higher expression-a heart felt need to sculpt SOUL . If the latter is activated during the act of intercourse i.e no emotional expressiveness, complete detachment from the feeling experienced then the karmic exchange is minimized as the emotional brain (its sponge like receptors) is rendered impervious to the exterior rant and frolic. Afterall, it is a procreative act, indeed Sacred, as taught in all the holy scriptures (east or west) but when the sleeping humangets a taste of the puncturing of the astral body (orgasm needn't even occur for the puncture to occur, Katerina) the lower expression of the emotional brain makes its mark: a forever, indelible mark that cannot be erased except by the intervention of the Holy Spirit and its COMFORTING TENTACLES, THE LIGHT RAY AND THE SOUND CURRENT! THIS IS THE TRINITY; THE TRINITY OF Father Son and Holy Ghost! The esoteric within the Exoteric; The microcosm within the Macrocosm; And finally: AS ABOVE SO BELOW ! ! That which art in Heaven is there for the asking, "SEEK and Ye shall Find." All above is the Legacy of the Christed Jesus; His invisible tentacles reaching down and through us bathing our being in the Grace of G O D THE ABSOLUTE ! ! !

So often I hear from women of all ages; they wishing they would have been privy to esoteric knowledge before they commenced a life with their chosen mate or any mate ! ! !

Tinker tinker little star,
Let the light shine down from afar;
Tinker tinker little star,
Let the melody echo its guitar;
Tinker tinker little star,
Let the Holy Spirit yield its nectar;
Lest we die with but a rage to live;
Simple Simple yet so hard for mind to give,

Tinker tinker daring Soul,
You penned the ink on Katerina's scroll;
She now imbibes her life long goal
To direct the weak who can't fare the toll,
The taste of venom, in life's harried bowl!

Katerina, another poem for you to ponder, hopefully, a
downturn from all that intellectual stuff you've been reading.

The Karmic burn off, His forte;
Watch watch for the light RAY;
Listen listen for the MELODY Today;
May the blessings of life candy your tray!

Katerina, Katerina, Katerina,
Worthy, worthy that you be,
May your heart climb the tree;
That tree of life by the Sea;
The sea inside, its waters flow;
Blessings numbered we can't know;
He is the salt that makes you glow!

You are You and Katerina is the robe
You wear with grace around the globe;
That is your mark this time around;
Fine roots you have clearly abound.

Listen Listen now for that SPECIAL SOUND;
The melodies vary but it is the KNIGHT,
Its armor shines, with tune of God;
He travels by the night
IT IS "T H E   W O R D "!!
IT CAN BE   H E A R D ! ! !
Listen listen now for that special sound
It carries Katerina and ALL souls around ! !

May the blessings be
As you swing from the tree;
Take a dunk into the sea,
For life is naught but Gaiety,
Or That, it Should Be ! ! ! ! !

The Work

I felt inspired to give Katerina some gift, a show of gratitude, for the
years of friendship, entertainment and evolutionary assistance. The
gift of learning (a starter library for your chosen profession) came to
mind. Whether you read them, now or ever, is your private knowing.
I know, heartily, you have been presented with advance teachings
that you could carry with you for life in your psycho-spiritual back
pack. I wish you the best  of luck in your psychological and spiritual
plight! You have just entered the beginning of your third Octave (21-
28yrs) a critical fount in one's evolution as Soul. You should already
know I'm available for questions you may have about the books.
Additionally, I have numerous related books for you to read.
May the Blessings Be
Ronne Gleason

Thank You
Poem

(Witty Commentaries on life's chess game of varied human traits; A living gratitude for each!)

Thank God for woman she teaches me kindness.

Thank God for Mom: Thank God for Dad: They gave me a
temple.

Thank God for woman she teaches me cunning, a weapon to
survive in a world of goats.

Thank God for Jesus, He is my light; He is my Sound!

Thank God for Spirit, She is my link to the bosom of God!

Thank God for the Saints, they teach me wisdom.

Thank God for Mom; Thank God for Dad; they teach me
affection.

Thank God for Woman she gives me inspiration.

Thank God for my brother he teaches me friendship.

Thank God for life it teaches me how to play chess.

Thank God for fine arts they teach me expression.

Thank God for soul its my vehicle to exit Hell worlds.

Thank God for friends they teach me giving.

Thank God for Jesus, He is my comforter.

Thank God for books they are my companions.

Thank God for me I am my friend.

Thank God for Mom and Dad they are my solace.

*Thank God for animals they teach me aggression.*

*Thank God for woman she teaches me softness.*

*Thank God for enemies they teach me forgetfulness.*

*Thank God for Business it teaches me self-reliance.*

*Thank God for husbands they teach me henpeckedness.*

*Thank God for divorces they teach me charity by not having*

                                            *children.*

*Thank God for hypocrites they teach me the virtue of simpletons.*

*Thank God for Fool-osophers they teach me the emptiness of*

                                               *words.*

*Thank God for suffering it feeds the moon.*

*Thank God for joy it feeds the sun.*

*Thank God for Marriage of the twain (sun&moon) it Borne the*

                                               *earth.*

*Thank God for spiritual healers they teach me karmic ignorance.*

*Thank God for astrology it teaches me anxiety.*

*Thank God for this Moment and only this moment it teaches me
the virtue in blindness to the future kindly given; given by God!*

*Thank God for gardening it teaches me slowness.*

*Thank You
Poem*

Thank God for seriousness it teaches me the virtue in comedy.

Thank God for hustlers they teach me stillness.

Thank God for "others" the teach me about me.

Thank God for smudges on the mirror it teaches me the need to meditate.

Thank God for dust it teaches me housebolding.

Thank God for criticism it teaches me non-identification.

Thank God for squirrels they teach me resourcefulness.

Thank God for birds they teach me song.

Thank God for magicians they teach me gullibility.

Thank God for Mom; Thank God for Dad; they taught me the blessedness of good fortune.

Thank God for parking lot dust; for parking lot holes; they teach me humbleness.

Thank God for Gleason and Associates it teaches me compromise.

Thank God for my marry-eds they teach about struggle for power.

Thank God for religionists they teach me somnambulism.

Thank God for orators they teach me shamelessness.

Thank God for presents they teach me generosity.

Thank God for drug addicts they teach me desperation (To Get Back To God.)

Thank God for Planners they teach me God has a better Idea!!

Thank God for children they teach me forgiveness.

Thank God for friends they teach me loyalty.

Thank God for politicians they teach me the folly of power.

Thank God for virtue it teaches me shame.

Thank God for crime it teaches me "we reap what we sow."

Thank God for philosophers they teach me hell is on the earth.

Thank God for Mystics they teach me Heaven is on Earth!!

Thank God for books they fill my head to the brim.

Thank God for meditation it empties my head.

Thank God for vegetables they give me strength.

Thank God for the Rockefellers they teach me futility.

Thank God for love it teaches egolessness.

Thank God for tennis it teaches me self-remembering.

Thank God for the early Church Fathers they teach me the value of asceticism.

Thank God for fingers they enable me to create waves that echo
muses from the organ in the sky.

Thank God for Mom; she made it possible.

Thank God for introversion it teaches me the value of organic
shame.

Thank God for the diplomats they teach me the shallowness of
personality.

Thank God for the forces of evil they teach me the urgency to
overcome the passions of the body.

Thank God for the enemy he teaches me the foolery of following
the flock.

Thank God for God's wisdom it teaches me I can't do anything
outside His view.

Thank God for making me a child, a benefactor of a near half
century marriage that is still going, it teaches me the virtue in
commitment.

Thank God for the unjust, for the lawless, they teach me to set up
post at the gates of justice.

Thank God for lovers who love the other first; their destinies of ill
fate teach me; Love God first; and grace will net them wine.

Thank God for a "good" mother; a "good" father; a "good" brother; And I'm sure their are many more; The tongue that chides either, the vultures of the sky will raze out their tongue and slurp the blood and the hawks will defecate on their corpse for God's creatures know stench from sweetness.

Thank God for lovers of lust and their suffering fates they teach me Un-chosen suffering is the road to hell fire; "chosen" suffering the sweet trek to paradise.

Thank God for diabolic women they teach me a slippery snake has a finer covering; in company with gnats are nectar compared.

Thank God for schemers their tillage bloated; They teach me sharks are friend –worthy compared, no bubble to burst.

Thank God for youthful women their voices paint angelic songs in the air; they teach me the tongue on my organ tune is pale in comparison.

Thank God for the saints;for the apostles; they teach me to die daily that I may meet their gaze on the other side.

Thank God for the Sacred Writings; they teach me; they teach me; May I drown in their bosom suckling sweet milk.

Thank God for the ancient Holy Fathers; they teach me the clothing of the earth; its fattened treats, are bagged in dung.

Thank God for the kiss of scarlet to white; the mystery Pink Dye; For your red drop, thanks mom; Four your white drop, thanks dad; You borne me into circumstances perfect for my evolution.

Thank God this; Lord Jesus Christ, son of God, have mercy upon my parent's even as they worshipped me in childhood.

Thank God for the evil woman and her barren opinions, they teach me [Less] than the rant of a day long dog bark.

Thank God for the Human word Coinage "Make Love"; it teaches me about the haughtiness of mortals who imagine they can actually make love.. Anything to polish guilt; skew sanctity and buff the emotional center. " God Is Love!" Can One Make God?

Thank God for those driven to get even, their madness teaches me the eye of evil trumpets vile siphoned through Satan's Jaws.

Thank God for the virgin woman she teaches me Satan has a weakness.

*Thank You
Poem*

*Thank God for calculating minds, thoughts hammered by indecision, they teach me a wrinkled head is folly; Trusting the heart is a mirror without dust.*

*Thank God for virtuous women they bring honor to any family, they teach me; they teach me; her tentacles stretch out and touch and touch and touch.*

*Thank God for the slanderers they teach me avoidance, for their verbal spears rebound back onto them one thousand times one thousand, churning out their bile for ants to suck; stay out their way to avoid the saber's strike.*

*Thank God for those deceived by the color of sanctity it teaches me that all are even pillage for Satan's ghastly snare.*

*Matthew 6:22 The light of the body is the eye: if therefore thine eye be single, thy whole body will be full of light.*

"Author channelling his sand garden"

# TRIUMPHANT SHADOWS
### (Emptiness Contained Within Carnal Treats)
#### 1972

Hapless times do swim cross-tide
Slyly badgering pursuits that abide,

Esteem to hush pleasures born of vanity,
And cramp the battle against insanity.

Enchantments fare and carnivals delights,
Sweeping the aura of fruiting sites,

Pierce the belly encircling the earth,
And rupture sorrow's well nigh to birth.

Sorrows buried, though that they were,
Emerged from deep, unable to endure

The tireless fleet of ecstasies barren,
And tantalizing fraud incited for darin'

To melt one's being into the kernel
Of pleasures base that market's the infernal.

Thorns now abound in noxious travail
Asserting their motion to accept the bail,

Erupt with venom in caustic robust,
And challenges the conviction, "All trials are just."

The valley of sorrow, woeful indeed,
Stampedes our days seeming to impede

Our gallant climb to the core of Peace;
'Oh blessed Jesus, we pray release

From sorrow's wake, its choke unfair,
And crippling despondency that cramps all care.

Sorrow's bridle frail from over-use,
Cannot be gleaned from thoughts hovering loose

Amid the Pandora of putrefacted dreams
That foster naught, but paranoic schemes.

The cyst of sorrow, if burrowed so deep,
Pampers self pity's clamoring weep.

The venomous splurge, now teeming our maze
That staggers your vision, insists we raise

Our blundering spirits to newly heights,
Lest we'll make stale all future insights.

Ere bitter the venom, ere greater the blessing,
For Heaven's cup, in spilling the dressing,

That recomforts souls in dire need,
Knows well the Pang of God's Fair Deed.

Thoughts so mustered, shall thusly enchain
Sorrow's relent and stalwart reign.

The circuit of Wisdom, strung from on High,
Endeavors to revive all blossoms that die.

The wayward spectrum, its vista so plain,
Else how could suffering exult the chain

That ever links a chaotic order
Beseemed to stray from its Divine cast border.

Scathing vainly, inviting friction,
Persisting for nil, but displaying fiction,

Taken wing to the phantom: Vexed times are constriction,
And sorrow and joy are morbid contradiction.

The acoustics of wrath, unshackled from above,
Now vomits waves that sample love.

Stripped of pride, the doubter's creed;
Sorrow's virtue, well guaranteed,

Shall dine, henceforth, a once tainted mind,
And spark a vision, both worlds are kind!

Freedom's spice now on the prance
Stymie's folly's upright stance.

Exquisite blends of rhapsodies approach
Abound the nomad's wayfaring coach.

The prairies contours, its fathom deep,
Embalms a spirit once fast to sleep,

As vials of wrath, their dyspeptic drink,
Empty wastes, well on the brink,

Of psychic paralysis's hypnotic greeting,
And stark opinion, "We exist for a beating."

Dereliction abounding; Freedom uprooting;
The scorch of nausea halts its polluting.

Reflections chaste, or enchantments wake,
Now fair to deem their godsend break,

Ushers the embryo vouchsafing the Christ
To infuse the spirit once morbidly enticed.

Personal conviction, bombastic prediction,
 Lays trace to Grace's stalwart eviction

From the froward's pomp, his tongue employed
 By the Prince of the earth, slyly decoy-ed.

God's propinquity, His solace un-spared,
 Inspirits the artisan to labor un-impaired.

Metaphorically reduced to hand soiling chores,
 Heaven's endow, the praiser of outdoors.

Poverty's chamber, the indictment for life,
 Crushes the poor, their faith in strife;

But Godsent grace, flooding the kernel
 Of spirits so stricken, shatters the infernal;

Erewhilst the creation of humility's stalk,
And the poor deeming it wondrous to even walk.

The chariot of the poor, so inflamed by God,
 Now traipse the earth, living off the sod,

And boast their joy mere necessities give
When the succor of God compels them to live.

Chance be well, an obstacle they meet,
 But share a joy they honor to greet.

Ousting with savor this country air;
Simply wondrous the environ calm
That rushes to my brain a numbing stare.

Chirps from animal life clear and concise,
So much so a symphony cannot compete
With melodies so foreign to city entice.

Through the lattice a rare type quest
Meets my eye; a comely deer
It tis that lay so unrepressed.

The rustle of leaves, when meeting winds caress,
Chastens the day with tunes that rest
For days and more earth-minded distress.

Glancing into the forest prow,
Wonderment breeds untimely thoughts
Of nature's might and free endow.

Uttering but whispers for your friend to call,
Replies begot so quickly it seems,
The country-like vista has built in walls.

The sound of quiet, its heavy-laden choir,
Taps a zeal for knowing the caste
Of my lady chosen virgin squire.

Frolic and care best left anon
So to compare my childhood play
With a country life I now dwell upon.

Surrounding neighbors to church they go
With hopes to live and hopes to die,
'Tis all I can say of them I know.

The rampant gorge of frail pursuits,
Exhausting energy to stem city strife,
Is brought to light by country recruits.

Looking headlong to blue-laden skies,
I viewed the glide of free-reined birds
That durst defies any sorrow to rise.

A flight from Care to splendors wreaked
From nature's tunes of timeless tides,
I bathed in waves that purely speaked.

*Retiring from labor, but gaining new life;*
*His cheer well fair'd for he'll be with his wife.*

*Sitting on thorns awaiting this day,*
*His goal is met with time to play.*

*Enjoying his job and working companion,*
*He'll carry their sentiments even to Grand Canyon.*

*His lively ways robust and just,*
*For he perks his men who confide his trust.*

*Departing ways of the working man,*
*He'll offer his person, and whatever he can,*

*To speed the gallop of a business plunge,*
*That exists to prove he's not a sponge.*

*Washed up for life, but surely instead,*
*To sweeten the aroma of past days led.*

*The years may creep, but so does Peace*
*That spices Nature's fair masterpiece;*

*Which is to harbor a successful sail*
*On lifeboat victory that now says Hail'*

To fruits of labor; Untie the bow,
And hear the rhapsody you were blessed to sow:

"Advancing years, though they bring tears
Over sentiments born, wish your fears,

And all like thoughts, to burn at the source,
And know your workmates will ever endorse

The times you afforded and concerns you gave
Despite your absence they shudder to engrave,

For looking in envy at your new pas-time,
They hardly can await their own due shrine.

Time on your hands to be your new lot;
Better fortune even shall be allotted

To you the VICTOR, who carved a fate
That will ever blaze the heaven-spun slate.

Sentiment's mood, frolic's wake,
The style of life you gladly partake,

Awaits your embrace to enjoy the feast
Relaxation invites and gaiety released.

Exploit the times and leisure born,
For freedom from the clock is yours to adorn."

My father fair and all deserving,
Shall hold your sentiments ever preserving.

Thus goes the rhapsody for SIR VICTOR DAD!
'Tis only the beginning for a new life to be had.

(Necessity for Shallowness)

In tune with Care I strutted along
The orange grove rows extending eyes
Through sun-baked leaves wondering it wise
To tend practical need all life-long.

The monetary world, its volatile market,
So callous to all who gage its way;
Ill-fates well deserved for wishing to stay
The whirling minds to feeble target.

Erelong I trembled while flowers of greed
Grew nigh to limit bespeaking my lust,
Or beseeming care for a future just
That lends no color to unquenchable heeds.

Sordid dreams, extended folly,
Soiling my soul is this  well true?
I'm not to know, this much I knew
For tides of heaven are marked finale.

Nowise, for circles of fortune to trod
I accept; their store for me I know
Is unerringly good lest the embryo
Of God's spawning-love is but a facade.

Bombarded by swarms of fleeting treats
Inducing nausea so sickening to me,
Roused from deep a thirst for Thee,
For the Lord His love never retreats.

Unmasking the trauma of worldly harvest,
I weighed effects of the accruing chain
Of streaming successes, well nigh maintaining
The devil's caress is an unwelcome guest.

Enraptured over mundane success
Bequeaths me to recall stories of old
Where fame and glory toppled even the bold
Despite the riches they did possess.

Exhausted from my thoughts of Care,
I commenced to reflect on not the fitting,
Though woe betide it t'was benefitting,
But gazed heavenward in high-wrought prayer.

To bathe beneath this gentle breeze
Dared chance me say 'tis this you never
Spoke to me of, else my endeavor
To close the book on Worldly sprees

Would well of been sooner, if not at least
To stem the rollick of a burrowing beast,
To bask my soul in muses released,
And usher the rays, my cosmic feast!

## 'Exquisite Intersections Of Ethical Imagery'

My love of words and their rich amber pump air in my mind on the cosmic wheel
While exposing my obsession with projective geometrics of the cosmic mind in the early seventies.

*Acoustics beatific; Acoustics beatific;*
*Un-restrainedly echoing the rhapsody*
*Of this our oceanic earthly auditorium*
*With such a galactic magnitude of*
*Celestial mechanics, and its all*
*Pervasive incandescent magnanimity*
*Of countless exultations,*
*I strutted gleefully down the borderland*
*Of an ever-widening Christ-Spun abyss.*

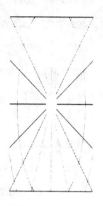

*The atmospheric accordion*
*Recording this terrestrial journey*
*Of musical Grace spasmodically,*
*It seems, jumps a chord to test*
*My strength in adversity, and in so doing,*
*Not only generates uncertainty in my mind*
*Underlying an ever-existent*
*Rhythmic regularity that colors*
*A cosmic pre-eminence or harmonic*
*God-Sent orchestration, but further,*
*Sweeps me into the wallowing pandemonium*
*Of an air-tight shell that drains my zeal*
*For Christian service to such a*
*Runinus degree, a once ruling passion,*
*Bows to paralysis, finding vent for the*
*Gushing trauma of self-born lust.*

Erewhile this Law of Divine Geometrics,
Seeming naught, but hollow groundwork,
The streaming lines of a rambling medley,
Intersect to form points, keys of notes
Of a creative symphonic scale,
That diverges to an infinite accountability
Of any chord once thought missed.
From whence originates,
In light of said analysis,
The reason why we are forgiven eternally,
And it is "Patience,"
(Realization of Timelessness
In space/cosmos),
That is needed by one and all for the
Groundwork of the pre-eminent Order
To be fulfilled and or Unreeled,
Devoid of our fettered observance.

Emerging from this net-work of a
Methodically spun web is the
Super-eminent necessity for constancy
Of purpose lest one shall stagger
Shuttlewise amid the already formed
Circuit of geometrically laid points
Giving vent to the ever-knawing incubus

Of skepticism, thus creating the
Nightmarish path of this hapless victim
Of self-willed Doubt and commencement
To servility to Demonic commands
All-while blatantly refusing to risk
Commitment to any of God's Geometrically
Patterned points on the musical
Web of destiny, hence the formation
Of lukewarm beings whose headstrong whim
To remain untied to God-Sent links
(Or points), displaying
A heavenly plan so well obviated
Per sensitive observance,
Our Bridge to eternal rest
Remains un-trodden.
Note: Rather than dangle within
(Unparticipatingly), an area of
Circumscribed points it is better

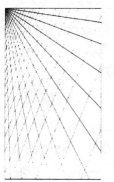

To cling to one of the points
(Become committed), "Hot Or Cold";
So that a conscience, good or bad,
(Granting such distinction at this point
Is essential for explanatory purposes only),
Can be implanted 'Deeply.'
Hence recollections after death shall
Consequently be much Clearer and Concise.
From whence we shall act and react to
Confrontations on or amid the astral plane
Of existence accordingly and more adroitly.

## Meditation 2

Herein, find the ever narrowing funnel
Of my past, present and future
Wherein circulates, viz a galactic
Centripetal force, the gradual peeling
Away of my obstructed molecular and
Cellular nature that diverges into the
Bosom of a centrifugally vibrating
Solar fluid of which contact affords me
Such ecstasy I find myself attributing
This union with none, but the
Blessed Jesus.
Enamored by God's awesome, but exquisite
Law of geometrics, whereby all lines
Meet their points of accountability,
I melted into the tearful,
But cleansing trials of repentance
Into ashes leaving behind me a
Mere echo of the stark
And hypnotic folly of
Worldly honors.

## 'ALFALFA SEEDS, THEIR DESTINY; TO SPROUT
(A metaphoric rendering of soul's human birth)

The sprouting of an alfalfa seed in a Glass Jar.
Image the seed lying at the bottom
(Genital region), of the glass jar,
(Physical temple made with human hands),
And clear glass (symbolic of where God can
See our auto-intoxication or every sin
Against our temple given us to purify).
Soaking and nurturing in the water's,
(Semen), used for daily rinsing or
Cleansing and further, the jar must be set,
For optimum results, in a dark area,
(Far away from demonic influences
As possible where they cannot see the
Fruition of Divine Working's),
And the opening, (Pineal center),
In the jar must be covered with a
Nylon stocking, (The little cap a Pope
Wears to protect his soft spot
(Pineal opening),
From unwarranted particles,
(Air-pollutants); the nylon,
Since it has numerous little holes to let
Air in to nourish the starving alfalfa seed
Is similar to the extreme sensitivity
Of the pineal opening, (few people only),
That allows the cosmic fluid to enter
And regenerate and / or create a newly
Potential sensitivity and receptiveness
Of the stems and leaves, (Ganglion-human nervous system)

## Alfalfa Seeds

Sprouting forth from the trunk,
(Spinal Cord), of the physical temple
Is the physical shell in which resides
The spirit of the alfalfa seed.

After this new receptivity or sprouting
Of the seed has enveloped,
The seed is then placed into he sunlight
To allow photosynthesis to instill
 Chlorophyll in the new-born sprout,
(Child), analogous to spirit meeting,
Spirit on common ground!
(Sun meeting the sprout viz-a-viz the
Nylon-symbolic also of the pineal opening),
And thus the creation of a third element,
(Trinity), namely <u>Chlorophyll</u>,
Which is the chosen regenerative element
The same as repentance is man's
Chosen regenerative element.
Henceforth is found that just as
Chlorophyll serves as the cosmic coloring
Of p h y s i c a l  i t y/plant so can man attend
To greener pastures-ideally taken here,
Per his reception of the third element.
More concretely, the third element
Is produced viz-a-viz our reception
And conservation of the cosmic - solar fluid, (SEMEN);
Which in turn re-activates the Ganglion

## Alfalfa Seeds

Or, (internal mechanics of the Sprouting alfalfa seed),
I.E. (The Nervous system of man), within the temple
Made without sound of hammer or hands.
And as we eat with joy
The fully sprouted alfalfa seed,
So does Christ eat the fully rejuvenated
And constructed fruit bearing,
(Sprouted ganglia), vines within**
Our human temple finally made properly
With the manna of God-Christ...

Hence my desire to share one of God's
Beauteous spectacles, the starving
And begging of a tiny seed that
Ever-graspingly reaches to the skies
For its duly Life On High
May the spirit guide you as you are
Audience to God's eternal supply of
Fruiting energies.

* For clear and concise understanding of the above, concentrate on the SYMBOLIC interjections
made evident by the **insertions in parenthesis, (***)** ..**Tree of life referenced in Genesis.

Dear John,

Away in the manger our Lord does lay, thence He rises from the waters and commences His glorious journey up the strait (not straight) way path to the region named Heaven and showers our being with joys of such galactic magnitude we melt into tears, expressing not only our sorrows, but our joys that come with being amongst the Saved.

May the Lord Jesus continue His inexhaustible and ever softening caresses upon your every tribulation.  And may your Mass with Christ be most merry every day of the year.

'Tis not the only season to rejoice over our Lord's kindness for all seasons bask in the loving caresses of our Lord.

Inspirited by our Lord and you John, I was afforded the great opportunity to materialize these thoughts and send them to your hoping they would tap even further the hidden love you have for our Lord.

I know indeed we need each other's admonishing's in our efforts to serve our Lord in a more discreet manner, lest our thoughts and past experiences and or trials would not have coalesced into an obvious similitude.

As you and I trod most joyfully down the ordered septenary scale I sense more and more a harmonic musical resonance that durst defies any and all negative or blasphemous thoughts directed to the efficacy and blessedness of our Lord Jesus Christ, and the Christed Jesus.

Jesus becomes Christed or Christened by John the Baptizer when we allow Jesus to journey unobstructedly to the church of Philadelphia, or Pineal Gland, whereby spirit thence meets spirit on common ground, (earthly Temple-Body), from whence embalming us with the shock of enlightenment clearly characterized by the nuclear explosiveness of the now rapid, top-like spinning of the pineal center-wheel or multi-colored Lotus, which in turn creates preponderant, tornado-like winds only auditory to our supernormal hearing.

I meant not to get carried away like this, John, for I do feel the letter should, ideally, be reserved for praising our Lord Jesus, and now that I intuit the unleashing of my pedantry I feel the proper turn to take is wrap this letter up in a knot, or Christ-Mass bow that can be un-tied only by you, and leave you with these seven words: Blessed Be Jesus, For He Blessed Us... Note SEVEN words spontaneously manifested...

Just sound the proper musical key or note...And lo! and behold the septenary scale of Sevens unfold.

Human Interest: Was the first thought upon the reading of this letter composed of seven words?  If you hit the same key as I it may well have been made up of Seven Words.

Joy Ever Profound,

Ronne

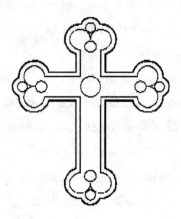

DEAR TOM,


BUSINESS IS YOUR <u>CARRIAGE</u>;
KNOWLEDGE IS YOUR FLAT TIRE;
ROBOTS ARE YOURS TO HIRE;
LOGIC IS YOUR COLLAPSE;
SPORTS ARE YOUR RELAPSE;
ARISTOTLE IS YOUR NEPHEW;
A SIGNATURE IS YOUR CUE;
MONEY IS YOUR AXLE GREASE;
RECEIVABLES ARE YOUR LEASE;
WORK IS YOUR CRIB;
CUNNING IS YOUR FIB;
AND FOLLY IS YOUR <u>MARRIAGE</u>!


WOMEN ARE YOUR KNACK,
MARRIAGE IS YOUR CONTRACT,
AND LO AND BEHOLD
THE BORNING OF A POLITICIAN
WHOSE SOUL IS SOLD
TO GREEDY MORTICIANS;


CARS ARE YOUR MISTRESS;
EGO IS YOUR DISTRESS;
BOOKS ARE YOUR FEAT;
SALES ARE YOUR TREAT


HEAVENLY PEACE IS MY TREAT,
AND A BUOYANT HEART IS MY BEAT!

Perplexed by a woman so fair to love,
Slighted by a man base as a dove;

Traveling the chambers of the soul
Unfolds the map of one lover's goal.

The organs of sex, in a woman they're concealed,
A miracle indeed, a child is revealed,

Telling her for certain there is more to life
Than the glories of the flesh, its reckless strife;

Here lies the cause of her appeal for the un-seen
And gift of intuition that inspires her dream

To tap the God-hood in her lover's soul
Trampling to death his childish goal

To seduce her and reduce her to a candied tray
While seeking admiration for his sexual display.

Hardly content to bring forth a child,
Or allow his godhood to remain exiled,

She conjures up an Ideal in infant years
Of a man to receive her love and cheers

Superior in some way to all his peers;
This is the direction she intuitively steers

While wavering between her world of dreams
And the limited world her man esteems.

Love to a man-child is sex to receive,
Afterall, his genitals are visible to believe;

Whereas, love to a woman is to create
Not only a child, but also the God State

In her man, whose potential she sees;
If a child he remains in his sexual sprees

She grows forlorn and weary to spite
Sensing rejection of her creative might

Cause he denies her pleasure in tapping
His God-Hood long ever trapped.

Women of the world, in seeking to be his equal,
Pave the way for a morbid sequel:

Already supremely inspirited to instill
The God-Hood in a man-child, her thrills

Have now been reduced to his level of fiction,
Borning in them a most crippling friction,

Her Ideal is marred and crushed,
A rage to die or passions flushed!

And this is a tale
Of a disenchanted lady

Her future frail
But a rage to live
For her man named ——————

(Ancient symbol of tranquility believed to actually calm the winds and breeze).

In time of quiet, in time of rage,
The gliding Halcyon still hoards the stage.

Content he flies, paving the path
On through the breeze despite all wrath.

Stealing space from his Fair-Wind friends,
He alters none the route they intend.

Space is space, to them its not,
Only to us, the greedy lot.

Does invasion from fellows alike
Painstake our pride we treat god-like

Eyes dripping wet in hot summer sun,
We fence off our space to boldly shun

Our neighbors stride, erewhile the Halcyon
Snorts our folly and flagrant con.

The tenor of his chirp, to change so drastic,
Should behove us to question our ways so plastic.

And fate, fairing righteous, bridle our lust,
Ere heeding a warning we should all come to
trust.

To appease the weary and worldly jury,
Our Fair-Wind Friend forgives our fury.

And choice to ignore the message he directs,
Knowing well the calamities we worship and
respect.

But Lo! 'a time may come when our forgiving
Seer portends us fugitive

To disaster's wrath and taxing wear;
Erewhile we mock our friend's despair,

And durst defy his omen wrought,
The web of destiny's unkind are brought!

Thus timely wallow in bloom to stay,
Rushing the flapping's of halcyon's at bay,

Remain time-short lest the melody
Cradlilng the earth, appearing in jeopardy,

Would bask in awe of the night-wind sigh
In search un-found of the sun-strewn sky.

Fairing well the temper sorely wrought,
The chirps of glee are welcomely brought,

Whilst I like not to prolong morning-wake,
And bathe in the dark a feeble in-take

Of rays, seven in color, born to heal,
And symphonic playing's halcyon's un-reel.

Amid the morning's hallowing breeze
Who abides the crest of my fruit-bearing trees

But the spritely gaiety of group-formed birds,
All eagerly in wait their food assured.

Pruning pride, our flowering beak,
Indispensable to yielding one's cheek

To ways self-sought so barren borne,
Forever remains our cardinal scorn.

In waste to lie, to bake it must,
Humility flounders, decomposing to lust.

Birth of an ecstasy, such wilt of virtue
Can well nigh bury the wisdom they espew

While during the pomp their graceful traverse,
Or atop the roof, caterwauling their verse,

Ever-comforts the guiltless submitting child,

While caressing emotions with titillations
                                        undefiled.

Tasks unblemished meeting rhapsody harvest,
Though doused with vexations they adroitly
                                        convalesced,

Harbored their labors, stoically victored,
And entranced by architecture, so artfully
                                        pictured.

The straw-cloven nest, its fluidic geometry,
So awed mortal eyes with its exacting symmetry,

It became the graven image to silence their
un-belief
Halcyons stirred by omens sent to brief.

Admonishing tunes from his dainty chords,
Faint to perish with his ill-fated swords,

So it did seem, sprung from deep
Enchanting chimes so long to sleep,

All future days were laden with signs
Of requiem's sigh and morbid inclines.

Alas the orchestration, its past filtering of doom,
Is raped of its raiment so tarnished by gloom,

Resting now in the bosom of celestial expanse,
Purging well, the Halcyon of ill-starred chants.

The pillar of Result, the pillar of Sorrow,
Its upright stance, still borders the morrow.

Despite the Halcyon's ill-omen casting absolve,
And gallant emergence into fair-omen revolve.

'Tis this our fate, to cast off not Woe
Ere-bright tribulation may appear to glow?

Well wise to heed, for peril's Fangs,
To grasp so pitiless with stalwart Pang's

May ravage the inferno of one's wearied soul,
Engulfing the spark that did console.

## A Friendly Halcyon

Like unto a Fable I cling steadfast
To enlightening melodies Halcyon's do cast.

And wiles of fate born to persist
Bow humbly to a Spirit they did resist.

Where lie the blossoms, so emerge the Thorns;

Where else to live in such high Adorn,
But amid stark-follies heavenly Born
Now harboring this earth I dare to scorn.

**The End**

If you are the king of the world; Lord of the screen; boast a house of gold; if base passions are your carry-on, then you're a passenger in flight to crash and have filmed before your eyes a new Royalty. I am now no more the King and I; I am now the King of death; I have gained the whole world; I have lost my soul! My body is now royal jelly for worms of the earth! Ah! the royal catacomb of death; a constant reminder to me how puny i am! And, who am I? Am I the motor, that fuels my passions, or the battery that lets the acid of God dissolve these knawing bites to death.

["Oh death! Where is Thy *Sting"], I know you can poke holes in the blubber of my passions, leaving unscathed, the kernel of my soul!

_____

I pray that even a smidgen of God's Will has colored my thoughts in penning these pages as we now live in profoundly degenerative wicked times wherein, the demons of lust, gluttony, IDOLatry and avarice seemingly ravage the core of one's every decision. For the young, please know that a life lived without self discipline, namely ascetic labors in the form of Fasting, Prayer and Holy Reading is tantamount to programming oneself to live and die like a common dog: [Hebrews New Testament "If you lead not a life of self discipline I will scatter your bones"]. It's easy to be liked by your peers (simply cower to the man-pleasing mind set) but not so easy to be respected by these same peers. A life of peer pleasing sculpts your pipeline to despair; despairingly trivial pressures. A peer for pleasure; Or a peer that's a treasure; May God gift you with DISCERNMENT that you may know your true Measure; Their true measure!

* It is written in scriptures of old, that the sting of death is equivalent to the sensation of being bitten by one thousand scorpions simultaneously.

For the Middle age male, if you have not yet reached your sixtieth year and fiftieth year, if female, please know that you still have enough sex power/energy to convert and transform IT into a golden furnace of flames QUICKENED to purge and burn away the base passions of the flesh. However, without Grace Given Awakening, not even the latter can occur as its predicate is aborting one's own Natural Impulses of the body! !

For the Aged, your sex power is to weak to convert itself into the purging flaming fires that could fry passions to death so the Holy Fathers of the Ancient Eastern Christian Orthodox Church admonish WORKING out your salvation by exercising the Moral Virtues to the highest degree; first by devoted study of the Holy Writings and scriptures, then acting out your acquired knowledge. Study the Visitor from Afterlife Poem, carefully, as you will uncover many-though they be coyly hidden, secrets of life after death. Also, consider the ancillary admonitions presented in each of the quatrains. May God bless you in your search. The afterlife is real; its terrors, and yes, all of its wondrous splendors, but only to the worthy.

May God bless us all; Guide us all in Voluntarizing our own evolution as Soul; our own Salvation, where the otherwise, hypnotizing effects of (so called) natural cravings surrender to our CONSCIOUSLY CREATED-DEVELOPED REAL WILL i.e. not a will formed out of a man-pleasing mind set [Ephesians 6:6 "Not with eyeservice, as menpleasers; but as servants of Christ, doing the Will of God from the heart;"] Let your false WILL be nurtured and carved out to perfection through intentional suffering and conscious labors. Intentional suffering attracts an easy yoke and lightening burden; IN-voluntary suffering attracts involuntary misfortunes!

Lord Jesus Christ, Son of God, have mercy upon my pen; mercy upon my soul; mercy upon OUR souls!

To those precious evolving souls who choose not to lead an ascetic life; a chaste and spirited life; then may you aspire to be Good Sons and Good Daughters to your earthly parents as one act begets the other namely, If you cannot be a good son; a good daughter to your earthly parents, how can you be a good son and good daughter to your Father which art in Heaven: A good Son and good Daughter to our Mother Of God, the Blessed Virgin Mary! ? ! ? AS ABOVE, SO BELOW IS THE ANCIENT MAXIM! Obedience is a secret elixir; drink from its cup; its tea anoints us all; its fruit fosters humility; its purging waters dissolve self will!

The T A O of Life: [T]ruth [A]bove [O]neself transforms itself into what seems on surface an endless interior struggle into a life as promised by Christ: "My burden is light and My yoke is easy."

**IF ONE'S HEART TASTED THE WINE THAT POURS
DOWN FROM THE HEAVENS EVERY SECOND
ONE COULD NO LONGER
(WITHOUT COMPUNCTION OF SOUL)
DRINK EARTHEN WINE!!**

*Orgasmic bodily love is one ounce;
Divine love is one thousand times one thousand tons.*